EVERYBODY'S FAVORITES COOKBOOK

The best, most requested recipes from America's churches.

Compiled and Edited by
Georgia A. Fisher

Communication Resources, North Canton, Ohio

EVERYBODY'S FAVORITES COOKBOOK

First Edition, 1984

Cover Design by Nick A. Betro Creative Graphic and Commercial Arts
Printed in the United States of America

ISBN 0-930921-00-3

Communication Resources
1425 West Maple Street
P.O. Box 2625
North Canton, Ohio 44720

CONTENTS

INTRODUCTION

It is the nation's local church newsletter editors who provided the inspiration for this special collection.

As church newsletter specialists, we have long noticed outstanding recipes among the thousands of parish papers we receive each month. These recipes were ones which received rave reviews at church events and were published by popular demand. As I collected these favorites from churches of all sizes and denominations, many began to grace our family table and some soon became our favorites. Thus was born the idea for publishing a collection of several hundred such recipes.

We invited our nearly 30,000 subscriber churches to submit the most requested recipes from the best cooks in their own congregations. The response was overwhelming. Within a few weeks we received over 1,200 recipes from enthusiastic church secretaries, pastors, and church newsletter editors.

Then began the difficult task of selecting a generous sampling of all the excellent recipes submitted. While the numbers made it impossible to kitchen test every recipe, each was carefully chosen with the assistance of a professional home economist and judge of numerous recipe contests.

I wish to express sincere appreciation to each who took the time to contribute one or more recipes; to Brenda Rapp who generously shared her considerable talents and experience; and to my family who, because of the substantial time and energy required for this project, learned to eat out a lot!

May these recipes add to the enjoyment and fellowship of your table.

Georgia A. Fisher

Appetizers
and
Beverages

APPETIZERS

HORS D'OEUVRES

1—7-1/2 oz. can crab meat
1 jar Old English Cheddar
   Cheese
1/2 t. garlic salt

5–6 English muffins
1 stick butter, softened
2 t. mayonnaise

Cut muffins in half. Blend ingredients and spread on muffin halves. Cut each half into 6ths. Put on cookie sheet and freeze. When frozen, place in plastic bag in freezer. When ready to bake, put in oven at 450°F. for 8 to 10 minutes.

Jean Pfeiffer, Arlington Community Church, Arlington, Nebraska

FESTIVE LAYERED DIP

2 cans bean dip
3 avocados
2 T. lemon juice
1/2 t. salt
1/4 t. pepper
1 cup sour cream
1/2 cup mayonnaise

1 pkg. taco seasoning
3 medium tomatoes, chopped
1/4 cup green onions, chopped
1—6 oz. can ripe olives, sliced
2 cups grated cheese
Tortilla chips

Layer: Bean dip.
      Avocados (mashed with lemon juice, salt and pepper).
      Sour cream mixed with mayonnaise and taco seasoning.
      Tomatoes, green onions, and olives, sliced and mixed.
      Top with grated cheddar cheese.
      Serve with tortilla chips.

Mrs. Bernice Ivie, First Assembly of God, Corsicana, Texas

SAUSAGE PINWHEELS

This recipe is used at wedding receptions, snack suppers, etc.

4 cups plain flour
2 T. baking powder
1/4 cup corn meal
1 t. salt
1/4 cup sugar

2/3 cup oil
2/3 to 1 cup milk
2 lbs. sausage (at room
   temperature; 1 lb. hot,
   1 lb. regular)

Mix dry ingredients as you would for biscuit dough. Divide into 2 balls. Roll with rolling pin into rectangular shape and spread on sausage. Roll up jelly-roll fashion and chill well. Slice and bake at 425°F. until lightly browned. These may be baked ahead of time, refrigerated and reheated at serving time. Good cold; best served warm.

Brenda Wills, Trinity United Methodist Church, Winston-Salem, North Carolina

HANKY PANKIES

1 lb. Italian sausage (remove
   from casing)
1 lb. ground beef

1 lb. Velveeta cheese, cubed
1/2 t. oregano
1-1/2 t. onion powder

Brown sausage and beef. Drain. Add oregano, onion powder and cheese. Keep turning until cheese melts. Spread on cocktail rye. (At this point you may put on a cookie sheet and freeze. Once frozen hard put in small plastic bags and store in freezer until ready to use.) Bake at 350°F. for 10–15 minutes. Serve hot. Delicious!

Delores Martin, Ebenezer Lutheran Church, Chicago, Illinois

HOT HAM SNACKS

1 t. prepared mustard
Dash of hot sauce

1 small pkg. cream cheese
1 small can deviled ham

Mix the above ingredients together. Cut out 2" rounds of bread. Roll a level tablespoon of cream cheese mixture in a ball and place on bread round. Flatten mixture leaving 1/4 inch around side of bread. Place in 450°F. oven for 5 minutes and then place under broiler for 2 or 3 minutes until brown. Can be made in advance. Place on cookie sheet and cover with waxed paper. Put in refrigerator and bake just before serving. Makes about 15.

Jacoba Schembs (Mrs. Frank), Wyoming Baptist Church, Wyoming, Ohio

TASTY MEATBALLS

1-1/2 lbs. ground beef
3/4 cup dried bread crumbs
1 cup minced onion
1/2 cup milk
2 eggs
1/4 to 1/3 cup brown sugar
(not necessary but adds a
good flavor)

1 t. salt
1/8 t. pepper
3/4 t. Worcestershire sauce
1/4 to 1/2 cup shortening
1—14 oz. bottle ketchup
1/2—12 oz. bottle chili sauce
1—10 oz. jar currant jelly
1/2—10 oz. jar grape jelly or jam

Mix beef, bread crumbs, onions, salt, pepper, milk, eggs and Worcestershire sauce in bowl. Shape into 1'' balls. Melt shortening in frying pan and brown meatballs on all sides, keeping separated. Remove meatballs and drain.

Heat sugar, ketchup, chili sauce and jellies until all jelly is melted, stirring continuously. Add meatballs and stir until coated. Simmer 30 minutes. Yield: about 100.

Florence E. Woelflin, Lorimer Memorial Baptist Church, Dolton, Illinois

DENNIS FOWLER'S SWEET MEATBALLS

2 lb. ground beef
2 cups soft bread crumbs
2 eggs, slightly beaten
1/2 cup finely chopped onion
1 T. minced parsley

2 t. salt
2 T. margarine
1—10 oz. jar apricot preserves
1/2 cup barbecue sauce

Combine first 6 ingredients, mixing well. Shape into 1'' balls and brown in margarine. Drain meatballs on paper towels and place in a 13''x9''x2'' baking dish.

Combine preserves and barbecue sauce. Mix well and pour over meatballs. Bake at 350°F. for 30 minutes. Yield: about 5 dozen.

Debbie Phillips, Jackson Park Pentecostal Holiness Church, Kannapolis, North Carolina

HASTY HOTS

4 green onions, minced
1/2 cup grated Parmesan cheese
6 T. mayonnaise

2 dozen slices cocktail bread or
    sliced French Bread rolls

Stir together onions, cheese and mayonnaise. Add more mayonnaise if necessary to make spreading consistency. Toast one side of bread. Spread cheese mixture on untoasted side and broil about 6 inches below broiler until bubbly and browned—about 3 minutes. Makes about 2 dozen. Serve and enjoy!

Barbara K. Willman, All Saints' Episcopal Church, Chelmsford, Massachusetts

CHEESE OLIVES

1/2 lb. sharp cheddar cheese,
    grated
1/2 cup butter or margarine

Dash Worcestershire sauce
1 cup flour
1 jar stuffed olives

Blend butter, cheese, Worcestershire sauce; then add flour. Wrap bits of dough around olives, put on cookie sheet, and freeze until hard. Bake at 425°F. for 12 minutes.

Barbara Emery, Zion Evangelical Lutheran Church, McHenry, Illinois

SPINACH BALLS

*Even children will like spinach this way. Lois' 4-year-old hated spinach but now **begs** her to make Spinach Balls!*

2 pkgs. frozen, chopped spinach
1 box stuffing mix
1 cup grated Parmesan cheese

3/4 cup melted butter or
    margarine

Cook spinach following package directions, drain. In large bowl combine dry bread crumbs and seasoning packet from stuffing mix. Add the Parmesan cheese and melted butter or margarine. Mix well. Add spinach and mix completely. Cool slightly for easier handling. Form into balls about 2–3 inches across. Place on ungreased baking sheet and bake at 350°F. for 5 minutes.

Lois Corbin, First Baptist Church, Manhattan, Kansas

ARTICHOKE DIP

1 cup mayonnaise
1 cup grated Parmesan cheese
8 oz. can artichokes, not
    marinated, drained

1 clove garlic, minced or
    chopped

Mix all together. Bake at 350°F. for 30 minutes. Serve with crackers.

Lois Mills, Christ Lutheran Church, Burbank, California

ZUCCHINI APPETIZERS

These appetizers are simple to make and delicious to eat!

3 cups thinly sliced zucchini
    (about 4 small)
1 cup Bisquick
1/2 cup grated Parmesan cheese
1/2 cup chopped onion
2 T. parsley, optional
1/2 t. salt

1/2 t. dried marjoram or
    oregano
Dash pepper
1 clove garlic, chopped or
    1/4 t. garlic powder
4 eggs, slightly beaten
1/2 cup vegetable oil

Heat oven to 350°F. Mix all ingredients together and spread in a greased 9"x12" pan. Bake until golden brown, about 35 minutes. Cut into 2"x2" squares and serve. This recipe can also be made ahead of time and frozen.

Marie Resetar, Southside Baptist Church, Tempe, Arizona

HOLIDAY MUSHROOMS

1/3 cup granulated sugar
1/3 cup vinegar
1 Bay leaf
1 t. salt
1 t. whole mixed pickling spices

2—4 oz. cans mushrooms
1—4 oz. can button mushrooms
1 small jar pimientos, cut up
1/4 cup onion, chopped

Drain mushrooms. Combine in saucepan: Sugar, vinegar, bay leaf, salt, pickling spices. Boil 1 minute. Cool. Strain. Pour over mushrooms, pimientos, and onions. Marinate 24 hours or longer.

Sandra Lee Rufener, St. Paul's United Church of Christ, Mineral City, Ohio

BRAUNSCHWEIGER BALL

1 lb. Braunschweiger	1 T. pickle relish
1 T. prepared mustard	4 oz. cream cheese
1 T. Worcestershire sauce	Frosting: 4 oz. cream cheese
1 T. minced onion	1 T. prepared mustard

Soften meat and cream cheese. Mix all ingredients together. Chill until firm, then shape into a ball. Frost with the cream cheese and mustard mixture. Garnish with sliced olives and chill until served. Serve with crackers.

Paula Sommerlot, Central Christian Church, Marshalltown, Iowa

CHEESE BALL

2—8 oz. pkgs. cream cheese	1/2 t. seasoned salt
1/2 lb. sharp cheddar cheese, grated	1/4 t. table salt
	2-1/2 oz. can deviled ham
2 t. grated onion	2 T. fresh chopped parsley
2 t. Worcestershire sauce	1 small jar pimientos
1 t. fresh lemon juice	1 cup chopped nuts (Save out
1 t. dry mustard	to roll cheese ball in)
1/2 t. paprika	

Mix all ingredients with electric mixer. Chill until firm. Form into a ball with hands. Roll in chopped pecans or walnuts. Serve on a platter surrounded by various types of crackers.

Rosemarie Barnard, Rinconada Hills Christian Church, Los Gatos, California

GRIFFIN CHEESE BALL

2—8 oz. pkgs. cream cheese, softened	2 T. chopped onion
	Salt
1—8-1/2 oz. can crushed pineapple, drained	1 cup coarsely chopped pecans
	1 cup finely chopped pecans
1/4 cup finely chopped green pepper	

Combine all ingredients except finely chopped pecans. Mix well; chill for one hour. Roll in finely chopped pecans. Serve with crackers.

Gay Bodine, County Line United Methodist Church, Griffin, Georgia

HOLIDAY CHEESE LOG

1—8 oz. pkg. cream cheese
1—8 oz. wedge cheddar cheese
1 cup ground or chopped pecans

12 drops garlic or onion juice
1 jar chili powder

Grate cheddar cheese and work thoroughly with cream cheese until it is smooth and creamy. Drop in garlic juice; work well to spread evenly. Work in pecans. Divide into 2 rolls; pour out half of the jar of chili powder onto waxed paper and roll one roll on the powder until all powder is used and roll is about the size of a silver dollar and 8'' or more long. Do the same with the rest of the chili powder and the other roll. Store in refrigerator and use as needed. To serve, slice in thin slices and place on Ritz crackers.

Mrs. Peggye McNeill, Reinhardt Bible Church, Dallas, Texas

PIZZA SPREAD

1 lb. shredded American cheese
  (Velveeta can be used)
3/4 cup salad oil, or more if dry
3 hard cooked eggs, chopped

1 onion, finely chopped
1—6 to 8 oz. can tomato paste
1 cup black olives, chopped

Mix together and spread thinly on bread, hamburger buns, English muffins, or whatever you choose and broil until bubbly brown!

Marlene Grimes, Covenant Baptist Church, Marengo, Illinois

PINEAPPLE SANDWICH SPREAD

15 large marshmallows
Juice of 1 lemon
1 small can crushed pineapple

1 pkg. chopped dates
1 cup chopped pecans
1 cup mayonnaise

Put marshmallows, lemon juice and pineapple in a double boiler and heat until the marshmallows are melted. Let cool. Add dates and nuts. Add the mayonnaise last. Spread on finger sandwiches or serve as open-faced sandwiches.

Deborah P. Massey, First Presbyterian Church, Covington, Georgia

CRAB SPREAD

1-1/4 cup mayonnaise
1 cup crab meat
1/2 cup cheddar cheese,
    grated fine

1 t. horseradish
4 T. French dressing

Mix all ingredients and serve with crackers. If you prefer a little extra tang, add more horseradish or French dressing.

Doris Ramsdell, Wesley Chapel United Methodist Church, Lydia, South Carolina

DILL DIP

2/3 cup mayonnaise
2/3 cup sour cream
1 T. dried onion

1 T. minced parsley
1 T. dried dill weed
1 t. seasoning salt

Combine all ingredients thoroughly. Makes 1-1/3 cups. Great for cauliflower and raw vegetables.

Edna L. Senoff, The Moravian Church of the Good Shepherd, New Hartford, New York

CURRY DIP

1 cup mayonnaise
1 t. horseradish
1 t. curry powder

1 t. tarragon vinegar
1 t. onion salt
1/4 t. garlic powder

Mix well and chill. Serve with raw cauliflower, zucchini, carrots, celery, etc. cut in small pieces.

Edna Bobbitt, Abney Street Church of God, St. Albans, West Virginia

PROGRESSIVE DINNER SHRIMP DIP

2 large pkgs. cream cheese
6 T. Worcestershire sauce
2 cans chopped, drained shrimp
1 cup Miracle Whip Salad
    Dressing

1 grated onion (medium size)

Assorted Snack Crackers—
    wheat and onion flavors
    especially good

Use beaters to blend cream cheese, Worcestershire sauce and Miracle Whip. Fold in onion and chopped shrimp. Chill overnight. Serve with snack crackers. For garnish, you can leave a few shrimp out to drain and place on top of dip with sprigs of parsley.

Mrs. Marylou Powell, Fowler Community Church, Fowler, Ohio

HEAVENLY FRUIT DIP

1/2 cup sugar
2 T. flour
1 cup pineapple juice

1 egg, beaten
1 T. butter
1 cup whipping cream

Combine all ingredients except whipping cream in heavy sauce pan. Cook over medium heat, stirring constantly until thickened. Cool completely. Fold in whipped cream. Serve with an assortment of fresh fruits. Makes about 2 cups.

Dorothy Thompson, First Baptist Church-Robinson, Waco, Texas

BEVERAGES

FRUITED ICE CUBE PUNCH

1 cup water
1-1/2 cups sugar
1 cup lemon juice (fresh or
   frozen)
1 cup orange juice (fresh or frozen)

1 cup pineapple juice (fresh or
   frozen)
4 qts. ginger ale

Combine sugar and water in saucepan, bring to boil stirring constantly until sugar is dissolved; cook 5 minutes. Cool thoroughly. Add fruit juices, pour into 2 ice cube trays and freeze. To serve, allow 2 fruited ice cubes per serving and fill glass with ginger ale.

Diane Copley, Fairview Baptist Church, Statesville, North Carolina

BANANA PUNCH

6 cups water
4 cups sugar
1—6 oz. can frozen orange
   juice (undiluted)

1—18 oz. can pineapple juice
Juice 4 lemons
6 bananas, mashed
4 qts. ginger ale

Place water and sugar in large saucepan. Bring to a boil and boil for 4 minutes. Remove from heat and add next 4 ingredients; combine. Freeze mixture in milk containers or pans. Remove from freezer 2–3 hours prior to serving. Add ginger ale.

Doris Ramsdell, Wesley Chapel United Methodist Church, Lydia, South Carolina

LET'S GO BANANAS PUNCH

2 regular pkgs. cherry Kool-Aid
1 regular pkg. orange Kool-Aid
2 qts. water
3 cups sugar

1 large can pineapple juice
3—8 oz. bottles 7-Up
3 bananas, blended well in
   blender

Combine all ingredients and mix well. Partially freeze before serving. If completely frozen, allow 6 to 8 hours thawing time. DO NOT ADD ICE! Makes 1-1/2 gallons (approximately 27 cups).

Becky Holt, Bethany Christian Church, Anderson, Indiana

SNOW PUNCH

3 cups mashed bananas
1 cup lemon juice
2 cups granulated sugar
2 cups light cream

6—7 oz. bottles of 7-Up
1 pt. lemon sherbet
1/3 cup flaked coconut (optional)

Beat first 3 ingredients together and chill. When ready to serve place mixture in punch bowl. Stir in light cream. Pour in 7-Up slowly. Add lemon sherbet. Sprinkle with coconut.

Lynne Biery, Christ United Methodist Church, Louisville, Ohio

PUNCH

1 pkg. cherry Kool-Aid
1 pkg. strawberry Kool-Aid
2 cups sugar

3 qts. water
1—6 oz. frozen orange juice
1—6 oz. frozen lemonade

Mix and add 1 qt. ginger ale when ready to serve.

Joyce Brinkman, Kingo Lutheran Church, Fosston, Minnesota

JELLO PUNCH

Excellent for weddings, showers, or school parties.

2 small pkgs. raspberry gelatin
1-1/2 cups sugar
1 small can frozen limeade
1 small can frozen lemonade
1—46 oz. can pineapple juice
2 qts. ginger ale

Ice cubes for punch
2 small pkgs. raspberry
  Kool-Aid
2 cups sugar
2 qts. water

Dissolve gelatin and sugar in 2 cups boiling water. Add 2 cups cold water. Add limeade and lemonade, mixed according to directions on cans. Add pineapple juice. When ready to serve, add ginger ale. May be made several days ahead; can be frozen. May be frozen into ring mold or ice cubes.

Betty G. Romine, First Baptist Church, Lake Jackson, Texas

PINEAPPLE SHERBET PUNCH

1—46 oz. can pineapple juice
2—6 oz. cans frozen orange
  juice

1 qt. pineapple sherbet
1 qt. ginger ale
1—6 oz. can frozen lemonade

Freeze pineapple juice in can. Remove 2 hours prior to serving and place in refrigerator to thaw. Mix all juices as directed and chill. Chop pineapple juice into chunks and put in punch bowl. Add chilled juices. Chop sherbet and add to mixture. Pour in chilled ginger ale before serving. This will serve up to 48 people. (Have also used raspberry sherbet for red punch.)

Debbie Phillips, Jackson Park Pentecostal Holiness Church, Kannapolis, North Carolina

GOOD PUNCH

1 qt. boiling water
1/3 cup loose tea
1 can frozen lemonade

2 cups cranberry juice
1—20 oz. can pineapple juice

Brew first 2 ingredients for 4 minutes, stir and strain. Add remaining ingredients. Just before serving, add 1 qt. ginger ale.

Betty Douglas, Church of the Straits, Mackinaw City, Michigan

IVORY PUNCH

1—12 oz. can frozen lemonade
concentrate
1—6 oz. can frozen orange
juice concentrate

9—6 oz. cans cold water
5 pts. pineapple sherbet
1 qt. vanilla ice cream

Combine lemonade concentrate, orange concentrate, and cold water in large pitcher. Place the pineapple sherbet and ice cream in punch bowl and pour contents of the pitcher over these and stir until sherbet and ice cream are fairly well incorporated into the liquid punch. Yield: about 5 quarts or 40 (punch cup) servings.

For a sparkling, tangy punch, you may add a 28 oz. bottle of ginger ale.

Dee Burton, Lakeview Baptist Church, Delray Beach, Florida

HOT PUNCH

2-1/2 cups pineapple juice
2-1/2 cups cranberry juice
2 cups water
3 sticks cinnamon, broken in two

1 t. cloves
1/2 cup brown sugar

Pour pineapple juice, cranberry juice and water into the bottom part of an 18–32 cup coffee pot. Place the cinnamon sticks, cloves and sugar in the top portion of the coffee pot, evenly distributed. Assemble coffee pot and perk as you would coffee. Will be finished when red light comes on on the pot. Serves approximately 25 people. Pretty and red and can be used at Christmas time!

Mrs. Judy Berry, First Presbyterian Church, Morganton, North Carolina

RUSSIAN TEA

3/4 cup Tang
3/4 cup instant plain tea mix
1/2 t. cinnamon
1/2 t. ground cloves

8 T. instant lemonade mix
with sugar
1 cup granulated sugar

Mix and store in tight container. Use 2-1/2 teaspoons of this mix to each cup of boiling water.

Mrs. Richard F. Mitchell, First Congregational Church, Hopkinton, New Hampshire

Breads
and
Spreads

BREADS

GRANDMA ADLARD'S OATMEAL BREAD
Used at Emerald Grove Church's annual Chili-Oyster Stew Dinner.

1-1/2 cups oatmeal
1/3 cup sugar
2 T. salt
1 qt. boiling water

2 pkgs. dry yeast
1/2 cup lukewarm water
8-3/4 cups flour

Stir first 4 ingredients together in large pan and let set until about 110°F. Dissolve yeast in 1/2 cup lukewarm water, stir into oatmeal mixture. Add flour and stir well. Cover and put in warm place to rise. Stir down when double in bulk. Let rise again. Stir down. Put into bread tins. Makes 3 loaves. Let rise. Bake at 400°F. for 20 minutes and at 325°F. for 20 minutes. Luscious hot from the oven or toasted.

Pastor John W. Eyster, Emerald Grove First Congregational Church, Janesville, Wisconsin

GRANNY'S SPOON BREAD

2 cups sweet milk
2 eggs
1/2 stick butter or margarine
5 T. sugar

1 t. salt
1 cup cornmeal
1/2 t. baking powder
1 cup evaporated milk

Heat sweet milk until it comes to a boil. Mix cornmeal, eggs, sugar, salt and baking powder. Then add evaporated milk. Add all to boiled milk and cook until it thickens. Put in baking dish and brown in oven. Add half butter to mixture. Put the rest on top. If mixture is too thick, add more milk. Cook 25–30 minutes at 400°F.

Viola R. Canode, Aldersgate United Methodist Church, Norfolk, Virginia

ANADAMA BREAD

7–8 cups flour
2-1/2 t. salt
1/3 cup margarine
2-1/4 cups very warm water

1-1/4 cups cornmeal
2 pkgs. (2 T.) dry yeast
3/4 cup molasses

Mix 2-1/2 cups flour, cornmeal, salt, yeast and margarine in a large bowl. Gradually add water and molasses; beat for 2 minutes. Add enough flour to make a stiff dough. Turn out onto a board, add rest of flour and knead until smooth and elastic. Place in greased bowl and cover. Let rest for about 1-1/2 hours until doubled in size. Punch down, roll and shape into 2 loaves. Place in pans and let rise again for 1 hour. Bake at 375°F. for 45 minutes.

Sarah MacQuarrie, Trinity Baptist Church, Lynnfield, Massachusetts

FRENCH BREAD

2 cups warm water
1 pkg. yeast
2 T. sugar

2 t. salt
5 cups (or more) unbleached
   flour

Dissolve yeast, salt and sugar in lukewarm water. Stir in 3 cups flour until well-blended. Stir in remaining 2 cups (or more) flour and knead until no longer sticky. Let rise 1 hour and punch down with fist; shape into 2 long loaves and put into greased pans sprinkled with cornmeal. (The long French loaf pans work well, but 2 regular loaf pans are okay, too.) Slash the loaves with a sharp knife 2 inches apart. Let rise about 1/2 hour. Bake 1/2 hour at 425°F. This simple recipe lends itself to experimenting with different types of flour.

Julie Morgan, St. Mary's Church, Hampden, Baltimore, Maryland

MONKEY BREAD

4 tubes biscuits (country or
   buttermilk)
3/4 cup sugar
1 t. cinnamon

1/2 cup nuts (optional)
1 cup sugar
3/4 cup margarine or butter
1-1/2 t. cinnamon

Cut biscuits into quarters. Coat with 3/4 cup sugar and 1 teaspoon cinnamon mixture. Place in greased tube pan (approximately 3 layers). Sprinkle nuts throughout.

Bring to boil stirring constantly: sugar, margarine or butter. Boil until sugar is no longer granular (about 2–3 minutes). DO NOT OVER-COOK! Stir well and pour over biscuit quarters in pan. Bake 25–35 minutes at 350°F. until nicely browned. Stand 5 minutes and empty onto plate. Enjoy hot or cooled.

Terri Scheil, The Christian Church, Estherville, Iowa

HOT PAN BREAD

1 cup flour
3 t. baking powder
2 T. shortening
1 egg, beaten

1/2 cup sugar
1/2 t. salt
1 cup oatmeal
1 cup milk

Sift flour, sugar, baking powder and salt together; cut in shortening. Add oatmeal and stir well. Add egg to milk and add to dry ingredients. Stir quickly. Pour into a greased 8"x8" pan. Bake at 400°F. for 35–40 minutes. Serve hot.

Vera Eubanks, Trinity Baptist Church, Lynnfield, Massachusetts

QUICK YEAST ROLLS

1 pkg. yeast
1 cup warm water
3 T. cooking oil

3 T. sugar
1/2 t. salt
3 cups flour

Dissolve yeast in warm water. Add oil, sugar, and salt. Stir to mix. Add flour and mix well. If too sticky to handle, add small amount of flour. Shape into rolls. Place in lightly greased pan. Let rise 45 minutes. Bake at 425°F. 10–12 minutes. Makes approximately 12 rolls.

This same recipe can be shaped and put into a loaf pan for a loaf of bread. Or it can be rolled into a rectangle and spread with butter, sprinkled with cinnamon, brown sugar and white sugar, then rolled up and sliced to make cinnamon rolls.

Very good and easy!

Elizabeth Lane, Baptist Temple, San Benito, Texas

VERY TENDER OVERNIGHT BUNS

1/2 cup warm water	1 egg
2 T. sugar	1-1/2 cup sugar
2 pkgs. yeast	3 t. salt
4 cups lukewarm water	15 cups white flour
1 cup cooking oil	

6 p.m.   Dissolve 2 tablespoons sugar and yeast in 1/2 cup warm water. Let stand 10 minutes. Combine in a very large bowl or dutch oven the yeast mixture with remaining ingredients. Work in the last of the flour with your hands but don't knead the dough. Cover dough and let it rise.

9 p.m.   Work the dough down and let it rise, covered, again.

10:30 p.m.   Work the dough down and shape into 60 golf-ball-sized balls. Space 1-1/2–2 inches apart on heavy greased pans. Work with well-greased hands. Cover rolls with dishtowels, then a heavy towel or folded tablecloth so they will rise "out" rather than "up." Let rise, unrefrigerated, overnight.

Next morning Bake at 350°F. for 15 minutes. Makes perfect sandwich or sloppy joe buns. The dough can also be shaped into cloverleaves or cinnamon rolls, with very tender results.

Mrs. Sara McClintick, Christian & Missionary Alliance, East Brady, Pennsylvania

BUTTERSCOTCH BUBBLE BREAD

24 frozen dinner rolls	1 t. cinnamon
3 oz. pkg. butterscotch pudding	1/4 t. nutmeg
(not instant)	1/2 to 3/4 cup chopped pecans
1/2 cup brown sugar, packed	1 stick margarine or butter

Butter bundt pan. Dump in frozen rolls. Blend pudding mix, brown sugar, spices, nuts in same bowl. Scatter over the dough and it will sift down between rolls as they thaw and rise. Cut butter into thin parts and arrange over top of rolls. Cover with towel and go to bed, leaving the covered pan to rise at room temperature. Next morning, preheat oven to 350°F. and bake in center of oven. Turn out on plate. Bake approximately 15 to 20 minutes until browned.

Jean Bushell, Holy Cross Lutheran Church, Dodge City, Kansas

MOM'S SWEET DOUGH

2 pkgs. or cakes yeast
1/2 cup lukewarm water
1 cup milk
1/2 cup sugar
2 t. salt

1/4 cup shortening
2 eggs
1 t. grated lemon rind
  (if desired)
About 5 cups enriched flour

Scald milk. Put sugar, salt, and fat into mixing bowl, pour hot liquid over them, stir well and let cool to lukewarm. Soften yeast in lukewarm water and add to other ingredients. Add about 2 cups of flour to mixture and mix well. Add eggs and lemon rind, if desired. Beat mixture well. Add enough more flour to make dough that is soft but stiff enough to be handled on a board.

Turn out onto a lightly floured surface and knead until dough is smooth, elastic, and does not stick to board or hands. Form into a ball, place in a greased bowl, grease top, cover and let rise in a warm place (about 80 °F.) until doubled (about 1-1/2 hours). When light, punch down. Let stand 10 minutes. Shape into rolls, tea rings or coffee cakes. Let rise until doubled in bulk (about one hour). Bake in moderate oven (350 °F.) for 30 minutes for coffee cakes, 25 minutes for pan rolls and 20 minutes for individual rolls. Yield: 3 coffee cakes, or about 3-1/2 dozen rolls.

Helen especially likes to use this dough to make HONEY TWISTS (this has been used for lots of bake sales).

1/4 cup strained honey
1/4 cup soft butter
1/4 cup flour

1/4 cup sugar
1/2 cup chopped nut meats

Form the dough into a long roll (like a broomstick) about 1'' in diameter. Lightly grease a 10'' iron skillet. Begin at outer edge and coil the long roll of dough around, leaving some space between the coils. Cover. Let rise until double (30–45 minutes). When light, spoon honey mixture *(but do not press dough as it will fall)* over the coils being careful not to let any run down sides of the skillet. Bake at 375 °F. for 20 to 25 minutes.

Helen M. Spangler, Eureka Presbyterian Church, Eureka, Illinois

GOLDEN HONEY ROLLS
These are great for Sunday dinner.

1 cup milk, scalded
1/2 cup cooking oil
2 T. honey
3-1/4 cups flour

1 pkg. dry yeast
1 t. salt
2 eggs (reserve 1 white for
    topping)

Dissolve yeast in 1/4 cup lukewarm water. Set aside. In a saucepan heat milk, cooking oil, and honey until warm. Remove from heat. Add 1-1/2 cups flour, yeast mixture, salt, and eggs. Beat 3 minutes or until well blended. Stir in remaining flour to make a soft sticky dough. Cover and let rise in a warm place until light and doubled in size (about 1 hour). Generously grease two 8'' or 9'' round cake pans. Stir down dough. Pinch off pieces with lightly floured hands and place side by side in a single layer in the pan. Combine topping and drizzle half over rolls now. Let rise again in warm place 20–30 minutes. Drizzle remaining topping over rolls before baking. Bake at 375°F. for 25–30 minutes or until golden brown.

TOPPING

1/3 cup powdered sugar
2 T. soft butter

1 T. honey
1 reserved egg white

Beat with mixer until blended.

Shauna Silcox, Good Shepherd Lutheran Church, Sandy, Utah

PIZZA DOUGH

1 t. salt
1 pkg. dry yeast
1-1/4 cups warm water
3–3-1/2 cups all-purpose flour*

*You can substitute one cup of enriched bread flour for one cup of all-purpose flour to add extra taste.

Mix all ingredients together and knead for a few minutes. Place in a greased bowl and cover with a damp cloth. Let rise one hour. Press onto greased pans. Add favorite toppings. Bake 425°F. for 15–20 minutes. This recipe will make two regular-sized cookie sheets. For a thicker crust, double the recipe and use three cookie sheets. Partially baked pizza freezes and reheats well.

Jan Hart, Church of the Nazarene, Banning, California

RING-A-LINGS

2 pkgs. dry yeast
1/4 cup very warm water
1/3 cup margarine
3/4 cup hot scalded milk

1/3 cup sugar
2 t. salt
2 unbeaten eggs
4 to 4-1/2 cups flour

Soften yeast in warm water. Combine margarine and scalded milk, stir until butter melts and cool to lukewarm. Add sugar, salt, eggs and the yeast mixture. Add flour and mix thoroughly. Cover and let stand 30 minutes. Roll out to a 22''x12'' rectangle on floured board. Spread half the dough along long side with Nut Filling. Fold uncovered dough over filling. Cut into 1'' strips, twist, and cover. Let rise until double (60 minutes). Bake at 375°F. for 15 minutes. Frost with your favorite powdered sugar frosting, using a little orange juice and shredded orange peel for flavor.

NUT FILLING

1/3 cup margarine
1 cup powdered sugar

1 cup chopped nuts

Cream margarine. Blend in sugar. Add nuts.

Jean Troutman, United Methodist Church of Matamoras, Matamoras, Pennsylvania

JAM MUFFINS

Great for church breakfasts.

1 egg
1 cup milk
1/4 cup vegetable oil
2 cups sifted flour
1/4 cup sugar

3 t. baking powder
1 t. salt
Strawberry jam or your
  preference

Grease only bottom of muffin tin, or put in paper liners. Beat egg slightly. Measure milk and stir into egg. Measure and stir in oil. Put dry ingredients into sifter. *Stir* directly into egg mixture, just until moist. Mixture should be lumpy. Fill muffin tins 1/3 full. Drop a teaspoon of jam in centre. Add batter until 2/3 full. Bake at 400°F. for 20–25 minutes. Place on wire rack to cool. Serve warm if possible. Makes one dozen.

Margaret Smith, St. Andrew's Presbyterian Church, Puce, Ontario, Canada

MARIE HAMILTON'S HOT CROSS BUNS

1/2 cup chopped candied citron	1 t. salt
1 cup milk, scalded	4 cups flour
1 pkg. active dry yeast	1 t. cinnamon
1/4 cup warm water	1/4 t. allspice
1/4 cup sugar	1 egg, beaten
3 T. shortening	1 cup dried currants/raisins

Soften yeast in the warm water, let stand 5–10 minutes. In large bowl combine sugar, shortening, salt, and scalded milk. Stir until shortening is melted, cool until tepid. Sift together 1 cup flour, cinnamon, and allspice. When milk mixture is tepid, blend in flour-spice mixture and beat until smooth. Stir softened yeast, add, and mix well. Add half remaining flour to yeast mixture, beat until very smooth. Beating, add egg, chopped citron, and currants/raisins until well beaten. Add enough remaining flour to make a soft dough.

Turn dough onto lightly floured surface, let stand 5–10 minutes. Knead and form into a large ball. Place in a dry greased bowl, turn to bring greased surface to top, cover with a towel, let rise again until nearly doubled. Punch down and form into a long roll 2'' in diameter. Cut roll crosswise into 1-1/2'' pieces. Tuck under ends to make smooth, round bun. Place buns 1'' apart on lightly greased baking sheet. Cut a deep cross in top of each bun with lightly greased knife. Brush tops with melted butter or margarine. Cover with waxed paper and a towel. Let rise 15–20 minutes, until light. Bake at 425°F. for 12–15 minutes. Cool on a rack.

FROSTING

1 cup confectioners' sugar	1/2 t. vanilla extract
2 t. milk	

Sift confectioners' sugar, mix with milk and vanilla until smooth. Brush buns with frosting while still warm.

Joan Errgong-Weider, Prospect Congregational Church On The Green, Prospect, Connecticut

BUTTER CRESCENTS

1/2 cup milk
1/2 cup butter or margarine
1/3 cup sugar
3/4 t. salt
1 pkg. active dry yeast

1/2 cup lukewarm water
  (110–115°F.)
1 egg, beaten
4 cups sifted flour

Scald milk and pour over butter, sugar and salt in bowl. Cool to lukewarm. Sprinkle yeast on lukewarm water; stir to dissolve. Add egg, yeast and 2 cups flour to milk mixture. Beat with electric mixer at low speed until smooth (approximately 1 minute). Then beat at medium speed until thick (approximately 2 minutes). Add enough remaining flour to make a dough that leaves the sides of the bowl.

Turn dough onto lightly floured surface and knead gently. Put into a greased bowl; invert to grease top of dough. Cover and let rise in warm place until doubled, about 1 hour. Turn dough onto lightly floured surface. Divide in half, cover and let rest 10 minutes. Roll each half into 12" circles, cut each circle in 12 wedges. Roll up each wedge from the wide end and place pointed end down on greased baking sheets. Curve ends slightly to make crescents, cover and let rise until doubled (approximately 30 minutes). Bake in 400°F. oven 15 minutes changing position of baking sheets when half baked. Remove and cool on racks.

Keithetta Mauder, Apostolic Bibleway Church, Linton, Indiana

BEST BASIC BISCUIT MIX

30 cups flour
1-1/2 cups sugar
1 cup baking powder
3 T. salt
3 cups powdered buttermilk *(do not omit!)*

7-1/2 t. soda
2-1/4 cups non-fat dry milk
6 cups shortening

Mix all ingredients except shortening. Cut in shortening until mixture looks like coarse crumbs. Put in tight container. Amount may be doubled or halved. This is a good mix for all recipes calling for Bisquick or any other biscuit mix. The powdered buttermilk makes the difference.

Elaine Lyda, Wi-Ne-Ma Christian Church, Cloverdale, Oregon

ANGEL BISCUITS

5 cups flour
3/4 cup shortening
3 t. baking powder
1 t. baking soda
1 t. salt

3 T. sugar
1 yeast cake, dissolved in
   1/2 cup water
2 cups buttermilk

Sift flour and dry ingredients together. Add buttermilk and dissolved yeast. Mix with spoon until all flour is moistened. Cover bowl and put into refrigerator until ready to use. Take out as much as needed. Roll on floured board to 1/2'' to 3/4'' and cut out (take a little flour and knead it before rolling). Bake at 400°F. on cookie sheet or shallow pan about 12 minutes or until brown.

NOTE: Leave them set awhile to rise before baking. The dough will keep for several weeks in the refrigerator.

Mrs. Gladys Freese, West Anaheim Baptist Church, Anaheim, California

BOHEMIAN KOLACHE

1 pkg. yeast
1 cup scalded milk, lukewarm
1 T. sugar
1/2 cup sugar
1/2 cup softened shortening
2 small eggs, well beaten

1 t. salt
3 cups all-purpose flour
1 cup cooked prune pulp
   (or fruit of your choice)
2 T. melted margarine
1/4 t. ground cloves

Combine yeast, milk, and tablespoon of sugar. Let stand while creaming 1/4 cup sugar and softened shortening together. Add eggs and salt to creamed mixture, blending well. Stir in yeast mixture, alternating with flour. Beat well and let rise until doubled in bulk. Shape into small rolls, or pat out on floured surface to about 1/2'' thick and cut with biscuit cutter. Make indentation in center of each roll and fill with a spoonful of fruit to which margarine, cloves, and remaining sugar have been added. Let rise until light, about 10 minutes, and bake in a hot 400°F. oven for about 15 minutes, or until done. Yield: 2 dozen.

Suzanne Hollenshead, First Baptist Church, Brazoria, Texas

FASTNACHT

2 cups milk, scalded
1 yeast cake
1/2 cup lukewarm water
1/2 cup flour
1 T. sugar
3 more cups flour

3 eggs
1/2 t. nutmeg
1/4 cup melted shortening
1/2 to 3/4 cup sugar
1/2 t. salt
4 more cups flour

Scald the milk and let it cool to lukewarm. Dissolve the yeast in the lukewarm water. To the dissolved yeast add the 1/2 cup flour and stir to make it a smooth batter. Then stir in the lukewarm milk, the 1 tablespoon of sugar and about 3 more cups of flour and beat smooth. Cover and set out of drafts in a warm place overnight.

In the morning beat the 3 eggs thoroughly and stir them into the risen dough. Then beat in the 1/4 cup of melted shortening. Mix the nutmeg, sugar, and salt next and beat them in well. The amount of sugar can be reduced if need be (Gladys uses the full amount). When these have all been well beaten into the dough, then add about 3-1/2 to 4 more cups of flour, enough to make a dough not quite as stiff as bread dough, yet still stiff. Cover the bowl and set in a warm place until doubled in bulk. Then roll out to about 1/2'' thick on a well-floured board and cut with a doughnut cutter or cut diagonal slashes to make small oblongs of dough. Let rise again. Drop them with the side that was next to the board uppermost into deep fat. Drain on brown paper and dust lightly with sugar and cinnamon. Makes about 4 dozen.

Gladys R. Kleinknecht, St. Paul's Lutheran Church, Mount Holly, New Jersey

ALMOND PUFF PASTRY

1/2 cup butter
1 cup flour
2 T. water
1 cup water
1 cup flour
3 eggs

1 t. almond extract
Powdered sugar glaze flavored
with almond or vanilla
extract
Chopped almonds or walnuts

Cut 1/2 cup butter into 1 cup flour. Sprinkle on 2 tablespoons water. Roll out crust to fit bottom of cookie sheet, ungreased. In pan melt 1/2 cup butter, add 1 cup water; bring to boil. Remove from heat and quickly stir in 1 cup flour and almond extract. Stir vigorously over low heat until ball forms, about 1 minute. Remove from heat; beat in 3 eggs until smooth. Spread mixture over crust and cover completely. Bake at 350°F. about 1 hour. Cool. Frost lightly with a glaze and sprinkle with nuts.

Diane Shick, Faith Lutheran Church, Great Falls, Montana

DANISH PUFF

1 cup flour
1/2 cup butter
2 T. water
1/2 cup butter

1 cup water
1 t. almond extract
1 cup flour
3 eggs

Cut 1/2 cup butter into flour, sprinkle with the 2 tablespoons water and mix with fork. Roll in ball, divide in half. Pat dough in 2 strips 12''x3''. Place on ungreased cookie sheet. Mix 1/2 cup butter, 1 cup water, and 1 teaspoon almond extract and bring to boil. Remove from heat and stir in quickly 1 cup flour and three eggs (one at a time). Spread over each dough strip. Bake at 350°F. for 60 minutes.

Top with powdered sugar icing and may choose miniature chocolate chips, nuts, coconut, sugar sprinkles, marshmallows, cherries or whatever you may desire to sprinkle over the top of icing. Can also use pie filling over top.

Pat Stuckey, First Christian Church, Brazil, Indiana

STRAWBERRY BREAD

2—10 oz. pkgs. frozen
   strawberries, thawed
4 eggs
1-1/4 cups cooking oil
2 cups sugar

3 cups all-purpose flour
3 t. cinnamon
1 t. baking soda
1 t. salt
1 cup chopped nuts

Stir first 3 ingredients together. Then combine all dry ingredients and add to strawberry mixture. Stir together and mix thoroughly. Fold in nuts. Pour into two 9''x5'' greased and floured pans. Bake in preheated 350°F. oven for one hour. A very delicious moist sweet bread.

Margaret Butler, Euclid Lutheran Church, Euclid, Ohio

BANANA NUT BREAD

3 cups Bisquick baking mix
1/2 cup brown sugar
3/4 cup white sugar
2 eggs

1/2 cup milk
3 bananas, ripe and mashed
1 cup pecan pieces

Preheat oven to 350°F. Mix all ingredients together. Pour into loaf pans. Bake for 55 to 60 minutes.

Charles Russell, Eastern Heights Church, Cleburne, Texas

ORANGE BREAD

Served at Circle Meeting.

Peel of 3 oranges
1 egg
3/4 cup sugar
1 cup milk
1/2 cup sugar

2 cups flour
4 t. baking powder
1/2 t. salt
1 T. melted butter

Boil peel in 4 changes of water until can be pierced with a fork. Cool. Grind and add 3/4 cup sugar. Cook until thick. Cool. Beat egg, add other ingredients (orange peel should equal 1 cup). Put in loaf pan (makes 1 loaf). Sprinkle orange peel on top. Bake at 375°F. for 1 hour.

Maxine Pihlaja, American Lutheran Church, Billings, Montana

APPLESAUCE NUT BREAD

2 cups all-purpose flour
3/4 cup sugar
1 T. baking powder
1/2 t. baking soda
1 t. salt

1/2 t. cinnamon
1 cup pecans or walnuts
1 egg
1 cup applesauce
2 T. cooking oil

Combine dry ingredients. Add nuts and stir. Beat egg in small bowl, add applesauce and oil and mix well. Make a well in the dry ingredients and add the liquid mix until blended. Spoon into greased and floured 8-1/2''x4-1/2''x3'' loaf pan. Bake at 350°F. for 50 to 55 minutes until toothpick inserted comes out clean. Yield: 1 loaf.

Mrs. David W. Jones, Eastern Heights Church, Cleburne, Texas

BEST EVER FRENCH TOAST

1 loaf French bread
8 eggs
2 cups milk

4 T. orange juice
2 T. sugar
1 t. vanilla

Slice French bread into slices about 1/2'' thick. Arrange into two 9''x13'' pans. Beat eggs, milk, orange juice, vanilla, and sugar well. Pour over bread in pans. Turn over to coat. Cover with plastic wrap and set in refrigerator overnight. Fry the next morning to golden brown. Serve with syrup or sprinkle confectioners sugar on top.

This freezes well and can be reheated in skillet or microwave oven.

Mrs. John F. Amstutz, Ferris Church of Christ, Vestaburg, Michigan

HUSH PUPPIES

1 cup flour
1 cup cornmeal
1 T. baking powder
2 eggs
1—17 oz. can cream style corn

2 t. sugar
1 onion, chopped
Chopped jalepeño peppers to
  taste

Mix together and drop in hot grease using a teaspoon.

NOTE: A small amount (about 1/2 to 1 cup) of chopped shrimp adds a unique taste.

Suzanne Hollenshead, First Baptist Church, Brazoria, Texas

GERMAN SOUR CREAM WAFFLES

4 eggs
2 cups buttermilk
2 T. sour cream
1/4 cup cooking oil

2-1/2 cups flour
1/2 t. baking soda
1 t. salt

Separate eggs and beat whites until they peak. Dissolve soda in buttermilk in bowl. Then add egg yolks, sour cream and oil. Add flour and fold in egg whites. Bake on waffle iron until golden brown. You might want to serve extra sour cream at the table for between the waffles. These are delicious with syrup or blueberry compote.

BLUEBERRY COMPOTE

1 can blueberries
1 cup sugar

2 T. cornstarch
1/2 stick margarine

Drain large can blueberries. Put juice in saucepan; add sugar, cornstarch, and 1/4 cup water and simmer, stirring until thickened.

Zuetta Putty, Eastern Heights Church, Cleburne, Texas

SOUR CREAM COFFEE CAKE

1/3 cup plus 1/2 cup margarine
2-1/4 cups flour
1/3 cup brown sugar
1 t. cinnamon
1/2 cup walnuts
1/2 t. baking powder

3/4 t. baking soda
2/3 cup sugar
2 eggs
1 cup sour cream
1 t. vanilla

Cut 1/3 cup margarine into 3/4 cup flour, brown sugar, and cinnamon until particles are fine. Stir in walnuts, set aside. Sift 1-1/2 cup flour with baking powder and baking soda. Cream 1/2 cup margarine in large bowl. Gradually add sugar; cream until light. At medium speed, add eggs one at a time. Blend in vanilla. At low speed, add dry ingredients alternately with sour cream (begin and end with dry). Spread half in greased 9''x9'' pan—sprinkle with half of reserved topping, spread rest of batter, then rest of topping mix. Bake at 350°F. 45–55 minutes.

Maria Bremer, Zion Evangelical Lutheran Church, McHenry, Illinois

SPREADS

GREEN TOMATO RASPBERRY JAM

Green tomatoes
5 cups sugar

1 large pkg. red raspberry
   gelatin

Put washed and cored green tomatoes in blender. You need 4 cups of tomato pulp. Add 5 cups sugar. Boil 15 minutes and add red raspberry gelatin. Seal in jars or place in jars and refrigerate.

Carolyn Clubine, First United Methodist Church, Dunkerton, Iowa

RHUBARB PRESERVES

Delicious on toast or as an ice cream topping

4 cups rhubarb, cut up fine
4 cups sugar

1 box strawberry gelatin
1 small can crushed pineapple

Mix rhubarb and sugar well. Cook on medium heat 8 minutes or more, stirring constantly until rhubarb is soft. Add box of dry gelatin. Boil 3 minutes more. Add crushed pineapple and stir well. Pour in sterile jars and freeze.

This is a nice way to use up last of rhubarb.

Mrs. Darla Ward, St. James Lutheran Church, Logansport, Indiana

MOM'S LEMON BUTTER

Grated rind and juice of
   2 lemons
2 eggs
2 cups sugar

1/4 cup melted butter or
   margarine
1/2 cup water

Combine all ingredients in a saucepan. Cook, stirring constantly, over low heat until mixture thickens to desired consistency. Serve with cake or bread. Yield: about 2 cups.

Rev. F.L. Huth, Jr., Faith Bible Church, Lynchburg, South Carolina

TOMATO PRESERVES

5–6 lbs. tomatoes (about 11 large ripe tomatoes)
4–6 cinnamon sticks, each about 1-1/2'' long
6 whole allspice

10 whole cloves
1/2''x1'' fresh peeled ginger
3 whole lemons
6 cups sugar
1/2 t. butter or margarine

Peel, core and dice tomatoes reserving juice. Turn tomatoes into a 5-quart kettle. Add the cinnamon sticks. Tie allspice, cloves, and ginger in a piece of cheesecloth and add to the kettle. Cook uncovered over medium heat until reduced by a third (about 30 minutes), stirring frequently.

Cut ends from lemons, then cut in half lengthwise. Slice halves crosswise into thin pieces, discarding seeds. Add the lemons, sugar, and butter to tomato mixture. Cook, stirring frequently, until sugar is dissolved. Increase to medium-high heat and cook, stirring until reduced to 4 pints (about 40 minutes). Discard wrapped spices. Leave cinnamon sticks in preserves, if desired.

Mabel Miller, Church of the Nazarene, Banning, California

CARROT MARMALADE

5 large carrots
2 whole lemons

4 cups sugar
1/2 cup nuts (optional)

Grind carrots and lemons (rind included), add sugar and mix well. Let stand in refrigerator overnight so a good syrup forms. Simmer the following day until carrot bits are tender. Add nuts if desired and store in refrigerator. Makes about a quart.

Serve on hot biscuits with a chicken dinner. Delicious on coconut biscuits.

Dorothy Thompson, First Baptist Church-Robinson, Waco, Texas

Soups, Lunches
and
Brunches

SOUPS

BROCCOLI/CHEESE SOUP

2 T. cooking oil
3/4 cup onion, chopped
6 cups water
6 chicken bouillon cubes
8 oz. pkg. fine noodles
1/2 t. salt

2—10 oz. pkgs. frozen broccoli
1/8 t. garlic powder
6 cups milk
1 lb. Velveeta cheese
Pepper to taste

Saute' onions in oil until tender. Add water and bouillon cubes; bring to boil, stirring to dissolve cubes. Add noodles and cook uncovered for 3 minutes, stirring frequently. Add broccoli and garlic. Cook for 4 minutes. Add rest of ingredients and cook until broccoli is done. Serves 12–15.

Phyllis A. Taylor, Rochester Christian Church, Rochester, Illinois

CREAM OF PARISIAN SOUP

18 oz. pkg. frozen vegetables
(cauliflower, broccoli,
carrots)
2 cups water
1 cup margarine
1 cup celery
1/2 cup onion, chopped

1 cup flour
4 chicken bouillon cubes
6 cups milk
1 cup ham, diced
1 t. pepper
1 t. Accent

Cook vegetables in the water until tender. Melt margarine in a skillet. Add the celery and onion and saute' until clear. Add flour. Stir until blended. Crush and add bouillon cubes. Add cold milk. Stir until thick and smooth. Add the ham, pepper, and Accent. Add the cooked vegetables.

Linda Hendrickson, Rochester Christian Church, Rochester, Illinois

ST. CROIX VALLEY WILD RICE SOUP

This is a favorite for Lenten Soup Suppers.

2 cups wild rice, cooked
(1/2 cup uncooked)
1 large onion, diced
6–8 large fresh mushrooms,
diced
1 cup flour

8 cups hot chicken broth (can
use chicken bouillon cubes)
Salt and pepper to taste
1 cup light cream or half & half
1–2 T. sherry or dry white
wine (optional)

Prepare wild rice according to package or basic directions. Sauté onions and mushrooms in butter about 3 minutes or until vegetables are soft. Sprinkle in flour, stirring and cooking until flour is mixed in, but do *not* let it brown. Slowly add chicken broth until all flour-butter-vegetables mixture is blended in well. Add rice. Season to taste with salt and pepper. Heat thoroughly. Stir in cream. Add wine, if desired. Heat gently but do *not* boil.

Gloria Haslund, St. Croix Valley United Methodist Church, Lakeland, Minnesota

HAMBURGER LENTIL SOUP

1 lb. ground beef
1 large can tomato juice
(5-3/4 cups size)
4 cups hot water
1 cup lentils
1 cup carrots, diced
1 cup celery, chopped
(include some of tops)

1 cup onion, chopped
1 cup cabbage, chopped
1 green pepper, chopped or
1 T. pepper flakes
1 t. salt
1 bay leaf
1/4 t. pepper
1/2 t. Accent powder (optional)

Cook hamburger in soup kettle until brown and crumbly. Add tomato juice and water. Add rest of ingredients. Simmer about 1-1/2 hours or until lentils are tender. Taste for seasoning as it may need more salt (Ruth sometimes adds a couple of bouillon cubes or 1 tablespoon Spice Island beef stock base). Remove bay leaf. Makes about 1 gallon of soup.

Some packages of lentils contain seed heads of a weed just the size of a lentil. These may be removed by putting lentils in a bowl of water. The weeds are skimmed out easily. It is not necessary to soak lentils. Canned tomatoes may be substituted for juice. Cut into small pieces. When in season, Ruth adds a cup of shredded zucchini the last half hour.

Mrs. Ruth Colburn, Manito United Methodist Church, Spokane, Washington

BEEF-VEGETABLE SOUP

2 lbs. beef shank with bone
3 qts. cold water
1-1/2 T. salt
1—28 oz. can tomatoes,
   undrained
1 large onion, chopped
1 cup green peas, fresh or
   frozen
1 cup potatoes, diced
1 cup carrots, sliced
1 cup celery, sliced
1 cup cut green beans, fresh or
   frozen
1/2 cup barley or rice, uncooked
2 T. parsley, chopped
1/4 t. thyme, crushed
1/2 t. sugar
Salt and pepper to taste

In large saucepot, place beef shank, water and salt. Heat to boiling. Skim off any foam that forms on surface; discard. Lower heat and simmer 2-1/2–3 hours or until meat is tender. Remove bone and trim off meat. Reserve meat and discard bone. Skim fat from soup. Return to saucepot and add vegetables, barley or rice, parsley, thyme, and sugar. Heat to boiling. Reduce heat and simmer partly covered 1 hour, stirring occasionally. Season to taste. Makes about 12 cups of soup (3 quarts); about 8 main dish servings.

May be prepared in advance. Cover and refrigerate up to 2 days, or freeze up to 2 months.

Mrs. Howard Voight, Pilgrim Evangelical Lutheran Church, Wauwatosa, Wisconsin

GREEN CHILI STEW

2 lbs. lean chuck or rump roast
1 medium onion, chopped
4 medium potatoes
8 green chilies, roasted, peeled
1 t. salt
6 cups water
1/2 t. pepper

Cube the meat fairly large and bring it to boil in a large pot. In another pan, cook potatoes, peeled and left in fairly large chunks, in salted water to cover. As the meat becomes tender, add onion, salt, and pepper. Combine potatoes and meat; add green chilies, chopped. Let stew simmer at least a half hour. Serve with fresh warm tortillas. Serves 8.

Arlene Schwab, First Church of The Nazarene, Chandler, Arizona

OLD FASHIONED OXTAIL SOUP (VEGETABLE SOUP)

2–2-1/2 lbs. oxtail or soup bone
1/4 onion, peeled in large slices
1/2 T. garlic salt
1/2 T. celery salt
1 T. salt
1 T. pepper

3 whole cloves
1/2 T. onion salt
4 carrots, diced
4 potatoes, diced
2 diced celery stalks
1 small bottle ketchup

Place meat in large soup pan (Dutch oven). Add enough water to cover meat entirely. Add onion and spices. Simmer on low until meat is cooked. Add carrots, potatoes, and celery. Add ketchup and stir slightly just to distribute ketchup. Cook until vegetables are done. A serving option is dumplings.

DUMPLINGS

1 egg
2 cups flour

Dash of salt

Add enough water to ingredients so that mixture just slides off a spoon. Make sure that soup is boiling and drop mixture into soup one tablespoon at a time. Cover and wait 15 minutes. Serve.

Denise Peterson, Arlington Community Church, Arlington, Nebraska

FAMILY SERVICE STEW

1-1/2 lb. stewing beef
1 large can tomatoes
3 potatoes, quartered
6 carrots, halved
1 pkg. frozen peas
1/4 cup red wine
1 cup sliced celery

3 T. tapioca
1 T. sugar
1 T. salt
1/8 t. pepper
1/4 t. thyme
1/4 t. basil
1/4 t. oregano

Combine ingredients in 3-quart casserole; cover. Bake at 250°F. for 5 hours. Serves 6.

Ruth H. Knoblock, First Presbyterian Church, Glens Falls, New York

CHEESE AND MEATBALL SOUP

2 cups water
1 cup whole kernel corn
1 cup chopped potatoes
1 cup chopped celery (optional)
1/2 cup carrot slices

1/2 cup chopped onion
2 beef bouillon cubes
1/2 t. Tabasco pepper sauce
1—16 oz. jar Cheez Whiz

Place uncooked meatballs (see below) and other ingredients except Cheez Whiz in large saucepan. Simmer slowly for about 2 hours. Add Cheez Whiz just before serving. Serves 4–5.

Can be done in crock pot. A little more water can be added if you think it needs it.

MEATBALLS

1 lb. ground beef
1/4 cup bread crumbs
1 egg

1/2 t. salt
1/2 t. Tabasco sauce

Shape into small meatballs.

Cleora Jeffress, Trinity Presbyterian Church, Mercer, Pennsylvania

EASY MICROWAVE CHILI

1-1/2 lb. ground beef
1 medium onion, chopped
1 small green pepper, chopped
2—15-3/4 oz. cans tomato
    sauce with tomato bits
1—15-3/4 oz. can chili hot
    beans

1 T. chili powder
1 t. salt
1 t. prepared mustard
1/4 t. garlic powder
1/4 t. pepper
1/2 cup chopped onion
1/2 cup shredded cheddar cheese

Combine beef, onion, and peppers in 3-quart casserole with microwave on high 9 minutes or until meat is brown. Crumble meat with fork; drain. Stir in remaining ingredients except last 2. Cover and microwave on high 21 minutes, stirring every 7 minutes. To serve, spoon into bowls, sprinkle with onion and cheese. Serves 4–6.

Barbara Willis, Grace Lutheran Church, Mt. Prospect, Illinois

A CROCK OF CHILI

2—16 oz. cans hot chili beans
2—14.5 oz. cans tomatoes
2 lbs. ground beef
2 medium sized onions
1 green bell pepper
1 t. garlic salt

2 or 3 T. chili powder
1 t. black pepper
1 t. cumin
Salt to taste
1 small jalapeño pepper,
  chopped fine

Brown hamburger, onion, and bell pepper in skillet; drain grease. Put in a crock pot. Add beans, tomatoes, garlic, chili powder, cumin, and jalapeño (optional), then salt and pepper to taste. Let cook for 2 hours or more. Feast.

Pat Barker, United Methodist Church, Wood River, Nebraska

OCTOBERFEST SOUP

8 oz. Polish sausage
1 medium onion
1 t. salt
1/2 t. thyme
1/4 t. pepper

1-1/2 lb. cabbage, chopped
16 oz. canned tomatoes
2 cups water
20 oz. canned white kidney
  beans

Cut sausage 1/4'' thick and brown. Chop onion and saute' in sausage fat. Add and bring to boil all remaining ingredients except the beans. Reduce heat and simmer 15 minutes. Add beans. Cook 5 minutes until cabbage is tender and beans are hot. Yield: 4 servings.

Mayrene Tucker, Northwest Church of Christ, Houston, Texas

SUPPER CORN CHOWDER

5 slices of bacon
1 medium onion, thinly sliced
2 cups cooked or canned corn
1 cup diced, cooked potatoes

1—10-1/2 oz. can cream of
  mushroom soup
2-1/2 cups milk
1 t. salt

Cook bacon in large saucepan until crisp. Remove bacon and pour off all but 3 tablespoons of drippings. Add onion, separated in rings; cook until lightly browned. Add remaining ingredients and dash of pepper. Heat to boiling. Simmer a minute or two. Top with crumbled bacon and butter when you serve.

Jay Hurd, West York Church of The Brethren, York, Pennsylvania

LOU SCHNEIDER'S CLAM CHOWDER

1-1/2 cup cooked, diced potatoes
1 medium stalk chopped celery
1/4 cup chopped onion
Salt to taste
Fresh ground pepper to taste
1/8 t. thyme
2—8 oz. cans minced clams, drained (save)
    (Shrimp or other fish may be substituted)

1/4 cup flour
3 cups milk
6 slices fried bacon, crumbled
2 T. butter
1/2 cup Cheez Whiz

In large saucepan combine: potatoes, celery, onion, salt, pepper, thyme, and small amount of clam liquid. Bring to boil and cook 10 minutes or until vegetables are tender. Gradually stir milk in flour and add to vegetable mixture. Cook over medium heat until thickened. Stir in clams, bacon, butter, and cheese. Continue to cook until heated through but do not boil.

Joan Siqurslid, Christ Lutheran Church, DeForest, Wisconsin

FISH CHOWDER

1 lb. haddock filets
1'' cube salt pork, diced
2 cups milk or cream, scalded

2 cups cubed potatoes
1 small onion, diced
Salt and pepper to taste

Cook fish slowly in small amount of water until it flakes when tested with a fork. Remove fish and separate into flakes. Cook potatoes in same water until tender but firm. Meanwhile, fry the salt pork slowly. Add onion and cook slowly until onion is golden. Add fish, salt pork, and onion to potatoes and fish water. Put milk or cream into onion pan. Heat and add to chowder. Reheat but don't boil. Delicious next day.

Ruth Wiley, Trinity Baptist Church, Lynnfield, Massachusetts

SOUPER SEAFOOD BISQUE

1—10 oz. can cream of potato soup
1—10 oz. can cream of asparagus soup
1—10 oz. can cream of chicken soup
2 cans half-and-half

1/2 can dry sherry or another 5 oz. half-and-half with teaspoon of sherry extract
1/2–1 t. dry ginger
1 can snow crab meat
1 can baby shrimp

Blend soups, half-and-half, sherry, and ginger in large heavy saucepan or crock pot. Heat slowly. Close to serving time, add shrimp and crab with liquids; stir in gently (One may also add a small can of salmon or flaked leftover cooked fish). Garnish with dab of sour cream sprinkled with chopped parsley.

Anthony Allen, First Congregational Church, Pasadena, California

LUNCHES

TUNA SURPRISE

10 English muffins, sliced in half
1 can cream of mushroom soup

1 can tuna, drained and flaked
Cheddar cheese, sliced or American cheese slices

Toast halves of English muffins in toaster. Combine tuna and soup over medium heat and warm through. On a cookie sheet, place toasted muffin halves. Top with a heaping tablespoon of tuna mixture. Top with sliced cheese. Brown in broiler until cheese melts.

May also be prepared in an electric skillet. Twelve halves should use all of the tuna mixture and serve 4.

Janet Goodman, Eastern Heights Church, Cleburne, Texas

SLOPPY JOE VARIATION

1 lb. hamburger
1 T. oil
1 clove garlic, minced
2/3 t. oregano
1/2 t. dry mustard
1/3 cup minced celery

1/4 cup minced onion
1/2 t. salt
1/8 t. pepper
1—10-1/2 oz. can condensed tomato soup, undiluted
2 T. ketchup

Brown meat in fat. Add remaining ingredients. Simmer until fairly thick. To serve, spoon over split toasted buns. Yield: 4 portions.

Juanita Cirillo, Hunton Baptist Church, Glen Allen, Virginia

BINSTEADS

1/4 lb. cheese (1 cup cubed)
3 hard boiled eggs, chopped
1 can tuna, white flaked
2 T. green pepper, chopped
2 T. dry onion, chopped

2 T. stuffed olives, chopped
2 T. sweet pickles, chopped
1/2 cup mayonnaise or salad
  dressing
8 hamburger buns

Mix ingredients together and put on buns. Put in oven at 250°F. for 30 minutes.

If made early, put in refrigerator and take out one hour before baking time. May wrap separately in foil.

Mrs. Lynn Lodge, St. Andrew's Church, Puce, Ontario, Canada

PIZZA BURGERS

2 lbs. ground beef
1/4 cup grated Parmesan cheese
1—8 oz. pkg. mozzarella cheese,
  grated
1 T. oregano

Salt and pepper to taste
1 can tomato soup, undiluted
1 T. garlic salt
1/4 bottle chili sauce

Brown beef, cool and drain. Mix remaining ingredients and add to beef. Spoon onto hamburger buns, wrap in foil. If kept in refrigerator, bake at 350°F. for 30 minutes. If frozen, bake 60 minutes. Serve with relishes and potato chips.

Joan Reinert, The South Church Community-Baptist, Mount Prospect, Illinois

BARBECUE SAUCE

Good for church potlucks or unexpected company.

1 T. margarine
1 clove garlic, crushed
1/2 cup ketchup
2 T. brown sugar
2 T. chopped onion

1 T. Worcestershire sauce
1/4 t. salt
1 t. celery seed
Dash hot pepper sauce (optional)

Melt margarine and crushed garlic clove. Cook 4—5 minutes. Add remaining ingredients and bring to a boil. Add sliced meat and simmer a few minutes. This is good with hamburger, cooked pork roast and beef roast.

Cynthia Mahnke, Ferges Free Methodist Church, Marion, Illinois

BAKED HAM AND CHEESE SANDWICH

Cooking oil or margarine
12 slices white or light wheat
   bread
6 slices cheese
4 eggs
2 cups milk

1 t. prepared mustard
Salt and pepper to individual
   taste
6 slices ham or the equivalent
   in ham pieces (Spam-type
   products also work)

Butter or oil a 9''x13'' baking dish or cake pan. Remove crust from 12 slices of bread. Butter one side of bread and lay 6 slices in pan, butter side down. Top each slice with slice of American or cheddar cheese (Velveeta is good, too). Top cheese with slice of ham. Top with 6 slices of bread, butter side up. Beat eggs, milk, salt, pepper, and mustard (beat like scrambled eggs); pour over sandwiches. Cover and refrigerate 8 hours or overnight if for use as a breakfast casserole. Bake covered at 350°F. for 45 minutes. Uncover and let brown for 15 minutes more (use broiler to aid browning if necessary). Let set 5 minutes before serving. Serves 6. The leftovers freeze very well.

Mrs. Bruce Wilterdink, Sandham Memorial Reformed Church, Monroe, South Dakota

HAM ROLLS

Served at wedding receptions and circle meetings.

1-1/2 pkg. dainty dinner rolls
1/2 lb. ham, sliced
2 oz. Muenster cheese
1/2 stick margarine, melted

1/8 cup prepared mustard
1 T. onion, chopped fine
1 T. poppy seed (you can use
   less)

Mix together margarine, mustard, onion, poppy seed. Spread on each side of rolls that have been split. Place ham slices and sliced or shredded cheese between. Heat until the cheese melts.

Peggy Reavis, Trinity United Methodist Church, Winston-Salem, North Carolina

BUN FILLING

1 lb. Velveeta cheese
1 can Spam
1/2 green pepper

1 small bottle olives
1/2 cup melted butter
1 can tomato sauce

Grind cheese, Spam, pepper, and olives. Mix with butter and tomato sauce. Fill unbuttered buns and place in pan. Cover with foil and heat in oven at 325°F. for 25 minutes.

Mabel Frederickson, First Presbyterian Church, Port Angeles, Washington

BRUNCHES

FANCY EGG SCRAMBLE

1 cup (4 oz.) diced Canadian
   bacon
1/4 cup green onion, chopped
3 T. butter or margarine
12 eggs, beaten
1—3 oz. can mushrooms, stems and pieces

1 recipe cheese sauce
4 t. butter or margarine, melted
2-1/4 cups soft bread crumbs,
   3 slices bread
1/8 t. paprika

In large skillet, cook Canadian bacon and onion in the 3 tablespoons butter or margarine until onion is tender but not brown. Add eggs and scramble just until set. Fold drained mushrooms and cooked eggs into cheese sauce. Turn into a 12''x7''x2'' baking dish. Combine remaining melted butter, crumbs and paprika; sprinkle atop eggs. Cover; chill until 30 minutes before serving. Bake uncovered in a 350°F. oven for 30 minutes. Makes 10 servings.

CHEESE SAUCE

2 T. butter or margarine
2 T. all-purpose flour
1/2 t. salt
1/8 t. pepper

2 cups milk
1 cup (4 oz.) American or
   cheddar cheese, shredded

Melt butter or margarine. Blend in flour, salt, and pepper. Add milk. Cook and stir until bubbly. Stir in cheese until melted.

Delores Martin, Ebenezer Lutheran Church, Chicago, Illinois

EGG CASSEROLE

For breakfast or buffet.

6 eggs, beaten
1/2 cup sour cream
1/4 stick margarine, melted
1/2 #303 can tomatoes, drained
   and chopped

1/2 green pepper, chopped
1/2 lb. Velveeta cheese,
   shredded
6 or 8 oz. ham, chopped

Beat eggs. Fold in rest of ingredients. Bake in a greased, flat casserole uncovered 40 minutes. Can be baked 30 minutes, then frozen; bake 30 minutes more when ready to serve.

Mrs. Eleanor M. Tweito, Redeemer Lutheran Church, Marshall, Missouri

WESLEY OMELET

Often served for Easter breakfast.

8 eggs
1 cup milk
1/2 t. salt

4 oz. ham, cut fine
4 oz. or 1 cup American
   cheese, shredded

Beat eggs. Add milk, seasoning, salt, ham, and stir in cheese. Pour into greased baking pan. Bake uncovered at 325°F. for 40–45 minutes until omelet is set and golden brown. Makes 4–6 servings. Serve with sweet rolls and fresh fruit cocktail.

Norma J. Stamets, Wesley United Methodist Church, Massillon, Ohio

MAKE AHEAD BREAKFAST EGGS

1 dozen eggs
1/2 cup milk
1 t. salt
1/4 t. pepper

8 oz. sour cream
12 slices bacon, cooked and
   crumbled
1 cup plus 4 oz. cheddar cheese

Beat first four ingredients and set aside. Melt 1 tablespoon butter. Cook egg mixture until set but moist. Remove and cool. Stir in sour cream. Spread evenly in greased 12"x7" pan. Top with bacon and cheese. Cover with foil and refrigerate overnight. Bake uncovered at 300°F. for 15–20 minutes or until hot and cheese melts. Serves 8–10.

N'Ette Gessler, First Baptist Church of West Allis, West Allis, Wisconsin

BRUNCH CASSEROLE

1/2 lb. bacon
8 oz. pressed ham
6 oz. mushrooms, sliced
   (optional)
1/4 cup butter, melted
16 large eggs
1/4 t. salt
1/4 t. pepper

1 cup evaporated milk
1—8 oz. pkg. cheddar cheese,
   shredded

WHITE SAUCE
1/2 cup butter, melted
1/2 cup flour
1 qt. milk

Fry and crumble bacon; set aside. Put mushrooms, ham, and seasonings in saucepan. Add white sauce mixture; set aside. In large skillet combine eggs, butter, and evaporated milk. In a 9"x13" butter-lined dish, place a layer of egg, the white sauce mixture, then top with bacon and shredded cheese. Cover and bake at 300°F. for 1 hour. Can be made ahead and refrigerated. If so, add 15 minutes to the baking time. Serves 12–14.

Louise F. Sanders, Central Assembly of God, Springfield, Missouri

HOLIDAY STRATA

16 slices day-old bread, buttered
1-1/2 cups cheddar cheese, shredded
1-1/2 cups Swiss cheese, shredded
2 cups cooked ham, chopped
1/4 cup green onion, chopped
16 eggs
3 cups milk
1/4 cup chopped pimiento, drained
1-1/2 t. dry mustard
3/4 t. salt
1/4 t. pepper
1/4 t. paprika

Cut bread into cubes. Alternate layers of bread, cheeses, ham, and green onion in buttered 9''x13'' pan. Blend eggs, milk, pimiento, and seasonings. Pour over layered mixture. Cover; refrigerate several hours or overnight. Bake at 350°F. for 60–70 minutes or until golden brown. Let stand 5–10 minutes before serving. Makes 12–16 servings.

This can be baked ahead of time and then warmed in microwave or oven.

Juanita Kendall, Grantville United Methodist Church, Grantville, Kansas

BREAKFAST CASSEROLE

1 lb. lean sausage
6 eggs
1 t. dry mustard
2 cups milk
6 slices bread, cubed
1 t. salt
1-1/2 cups cheese, shredded
4 oz. mushroom pieces (optional)

Brown sausage; drain and cool. Beat eggs and milk together. Add salt and mustard, and beat again. Add bread and stir until it softens. Stir in cheese, mushrooms, and sausage. Pour into greased 9''x13'' pan and refrigerate overnight. Bake in a 350°F. oven 40–45 minutes. Let stand for a few minutes before cutting. Serves 6. Serve for brunch with a dish of fresh fruits and coffee cake.

Mrs. Mildred Knosher, Bethany Lutheran Church, Naperville, Illinois

QUICHE LORRAINE

Pastry for 9'' one-crust pie
8 slices bacon (about 1/2 lb.),
   crisply fried and crumbled
1-1/2 cups Swiss cheese,
   shredded
1/3 cup onions, minced

4 eggs
2 cups whipping cream
1/4 t. salt
1/4 t. sugar
1/8 t. cayenne red pepper
1/2 t. powdered mustard

Heat oven to 425°F. Prepare pastry. Sprinkle bacon, cheese, and onions in pastry-lined pie pan. Beat eggs slightly. Beat in remaining ingredients. Pour cream mixture into pie pan. Bake 15 minutes. Reduce oven temperature to 300°F. and bake for 30 minutes longer or until knife inserted 1'' from edge comes out clean. Let stand for 10 minutes. Cut in wedges and serve.

Charles Russell, Eastern Heights Church, Cleburne, Texas

IMPOSSIBLE QUICHE

Everyone will ask for this tasty and satisfying dish.

1 small can mushrooms
1—16 oz. can La Choy chop
   suey vegetables
1 cup ham or chicken, chopped
   and cooked
1—4 oz. cup cheese, shredded

1-1/2 cups milk
3/4 cup Bisquick
3 eggs
Salt and pepper
1/2 cup onion (optional)

Sprinkle chop suey vegetables, mushrooms, ham or chicken, and cheese in a deep 10'' pie plate. Blend milk, Bisquick, eggs, salt and pepper (to taste) for 15 seconds at high speed. Pour over the above. Bake in preheated 400°F. oven for approximately 30 minutes. Remove from oven and let stand 5 minutes. Cut in wedges and serve.

Mrs. Vaughn (Virginia) Sherman, United Methodist Church of Oak Harbor, Oak Harbor, Ohio

Salads
and
Dressings

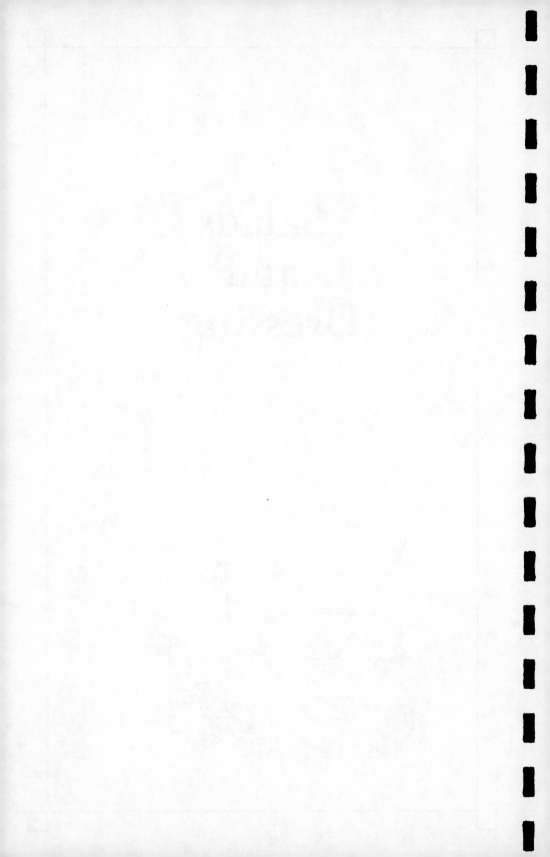

SALADS

FROZEN SALAD

1—8 oz. pkg. cream cheese
3/4 cup sugar
1—8 oz. can pineapple
1—10 oz. pkg. frozen strawberries

2—4 bananas, sliced
1/2 cup nuts, chopped
1 large carton Cool Whip

Blend softened cream cheese with sugar, preferably in mixer. Stir in fruit until well blended. Fold in nuts and Cool Whip. Pour into your prettiest glass bowl and freeze.

Will keep several weeks if well frozen. Makes a large salad or put in two bowls to use one and freeze the other for later.

Irene Cortez, Wichita Seventh-day Adventist-South Church, Wichita, Kansas

STRAWBERRY SALAD

1—10 oz. pkg. frozen
   strawberries
1—8 oz. pkg. cream cheese
3/4 cup sugar

1 large can pineapple, drained
2 bananas, diced
1 cup pecans, chopped
1 large tub Cool Whip

Cream cream cheese and sugar with mixer. Fold in remaining ingredients, ending with Cool Whip. Refrigerate. Delicious!

Mrs. Ginger Bush, First Assembly of God, Franklin, North Carolina

TEXAS WALDORF SALAD

2 cups apples, diced
2 T. lemon juice
1 t. sugar
1/2 cup mayonnaise
1/4 cup milk, mixed with 1 T. sugar

1 cup celery, thinly sliced
1/2 cup walnuts, broken
1 cup marshmallows

Toss diced apples with lemon juice, sugar, and 1 tablespoon mayonnaise, mixed together. Mix until well coated. Add remaining ingredients. Serve.

Mrs. Peggye McNeill, Reinhardt Bible Church, Dallas, Texas

BANANA NUT SALAD

2 cups pineapple juice
1 cup sugar
1/2 cup flour
2 eggs

2 T. vinegar
Bananas
Spanish peanuts, crushed

Mix the first 5 ingredients and place on medium heat. Cook until it thickens. Let cool. When cooled, put layer of sauce, then layer of bananas, then layer of crushed peanuts. Repeat this until all gone (ending with sauce). Refrigerate and serve.

Pat Stuckey, First Christian Church, Brazil, Indiana

PINK ARCTIC FROZEN FRUIT SALAD

1—8 oz. pkg. cream cheese
2 T. mayonnaise
1—8 oz. can whole cranberry
  sauce

1 cup crushed pineapple, drained
1/2 cup English walnuts or
  pecans, chopped
1 cup prepared Dream Whip

Soften cream cheese. Blend with mayonnaise, sugar, cranberry sauce, crushed pineapple, and nuts. Fold in Dream Whip. Place paper muffin cups in muffin tins and fill with salad mixture; freeze. When frozen, they can be placed in a plastic bag and kept in freezer until ready to use. Makes 8–10.

Emmie Mayhand, St. Thomas Episcopal Church, Columbus, Georgia

GRAMMA'S BEST CRANBERRY SALAD

Great for Thanksgiving!

1 lb. cranberries, coarsely
  ground
2 cups sugar
1 orange skin, grated, then use
  juice

2 small boxes or 1 family size
  lemon gelatin
1/2 cup nuts, chopped coarse
1/2 cup celery, chopped

Combine first 3 ingredients. Set aside. Mix gelatin as directed on package. Chill until almost firm, then mix together cranberry mixture, celery, and nuts. Use well-oiled mold or 9"x13" pan. Chill until firm. Serve on lettuce beds.

Alicia Bigalow, First United Methodist Church, St. Cloud, Florida

CRANORANGE APPLE SALAD

2—3 oz. or 1—6 oz. raspberry
  gelatin
2 cups boiling water
1 envelope Knox gelatin,
  dissolved in 1 T. lemon
  juice

1/2 cup cold water
2—14 oz. jars Ocean Spray
  CranOrange sauce
1 cup mayonnaise
2 medium apples, peeled, finely
  diced (about 1-1/2 cups)

In a large bowl dissolve gelatin in the boiling water. Stir in the Knox gelatin. Stir in the 2 jars CranOrange sauce; stir in the cold water. Chill until partially set, stirring with a fork a couple times. Beat in the mayonnaise (rotary or electric mixer is fine). Stir in the apples. Pour into a prepared 9"x13" pan or mold. Chill until serving time. May be made a day ahead. Serves 12–15.

Patty Anderson, First Presbyterian Church, Woodburn, Oregon

HEAVENLY ORANGE FLUFF

Served at United Methodist Women's Spring Salad Suppers.

2 pkgs. orange gelatin
2 cups hot water
1 small can frozen orange juice,
  undiluted

1–2 small cans mandarin
  oranges
1 large can crushed pineapple,
  not drained

Mix gelatin with hot water. Stir in undiluted orange juice; cool. Add oranges and pineapple to gelatin mixture. Pour in 13"x11" dish and congeal.

TOPPING
1 pkg. instant lemon pudding
1 cup milk

1/2 pt. whipping cream

Beat pudding with milk until slightly firm. Whip cream (use Dream Whip or whipped topping if desired). Fold into pudding mixture. Spread on gelatin. May be served in square on lettuce.

This topping has a variety of uses on other gelatin flavors.

Mary Hege, Trinity United Methodist Church, Winston-Salem, North Carolina

7-UP SALAD

1 pkg. lime gelatin
1 pkg. lemon gelatin
2 cups 7-Up

1 cup miniature marshmallows
2 large bananas, sliced
1 cup pineapple, drained

Dissolve the two packages of gelatin in 2 cups boiling water; add 7-Up. When partially congealed, add the remaining ingredients and pour in a 9''x13'' pan. Let chill.

Lonne Kay Mackie, First United Methodist Church, Blair, Nebraska

LIFESAVER GELATIN SALAD

1 small pkg. orange-pineapple
    gelatin
1-1/2 cups boiling water
1 cup cabbage, finely shredded
1 cup celery, chopped very
    small
1 large apple, cut in small cubes

1 small carrot, grated
1 small can crushed pineapple,
    drain and save juice
1 cup nuts, finely chopped
2-1/2 liberal T. mayonnaise
    (do not use salad dressing)

Pour hot water over gelatin. Add 1/2 cup pineapple juice; dissolve and refrigerate. Mix vegetables, fruit, nuts, and mayonnaise. Chill. When gelatin has reached a jelly stage, fold in the chilled mixture. Pour in large mold or small ones and chill until set (about 2 hours).

Harriette Colvin, Grace Community Church, Ramona, California

PINEAPPLE-CHEESE CONGEALED SALAD

1—6 oz. pkg. lemon gelatin
2 cups boiling water
1—6 oz. can evaporated milk
4 T. mayonnaise

1—16 oz. can crushed
    pineapple with juice
1-1/2 cups cheese, grated
    (Velveeta or cheddar cheese)

Dissolve gelatin in 2 cups (16 ounces) boiling water. Let stand 10 minutes. Add remaining ingredients. Pour into large casserole or glass dish and place in refrigerator until ready to serve. Serves 10–12 people.

Mrs. Berta S. Oliver, Main Post Catholic Chapel, Fort Benning, Georgia

CHERRY SALAD

2—3 oz. pkg. cherry gelatin   1 can cherry pie filling
2 cups hot water

Dissolve gelatin in hot water. Stir in pie filling. Turn into 9''x9'' cake dish. Chill until set.

TOPPING

12 large marshmallows   1 cup whipped cream
1—3 oz. pkg. cream cheese

Melt marshmallows and combine with cream cheese. When blended and cool, fold in whipped cream. Spread over gelatin mixture.

Jean Bushell, Holy Cross Lutheran Church, Dodge City, Kansas

THE SECRET POTATO SALAD

2-1/2 lbs. potatoes   5–6 eggs, hard boiled and cool
1 t. sugar   1-1/2 cups celery, diced
1 t. dry mustard   1/2 cup onion, diced finely
2 cups Miracle Whip

Boil the potatoes in their jackets in salted water. When done, drain well and leave at room temperature until completely cooled *(Do not refrigerate at this time or use potatoes that have been refrigerated)*. When potatoes are cool, peel and dice into large bowl; salt and pepper generously, or to taste. Sprinkle with sugar and dry mustard. Add 1 cup Miracle Whip, mix well, and let set while preparing vegetables. Add the celery, onions, and diced eggs to the potatoes with another cup of Miracle Whip. Mix well. *Now it should be refrigerated!*

Lucie Smellie, Eureka Presbyterian Church, Eureka, Illinois

HOT GERMAN POTATO SALAD

Requested every year for church picnic.

6 lbs. potatoes   1/2 cup sugar
1 lb. bacon   1/2 pkg. dry (Good Seasons)
2 bunches green onions   garlic salad dressing mix
3 T. flour   1-1/2 cups water
1-1/4 cups vinegar

Cook and dice potatoes. Fry the bacon and pour off half (or less) of the grease. Add the chopped green onions (green tops also) and fry slightly. Mix the flour, vinegar, sugar, seasoning, and water. Pour mixture over potatoes and bake at 300 °F. for 1 hour. Sprinkle with paprika. Uncover the last 15 minutes.

Verna Bierle, First Congregational Church UCC, Webster City, Iowa

MACARONI SALAD

3 cups macaroni, uncooked
measure
1 medium onion, chopped
1/2 cup celery, chopped
1 medium green pepper,
chopped

3 hard boiled eggs, mashed
3 cups mayonnaise
3 T. prepared mustard
1 t. salt
1/2 cup sugar

Combine mashed eggs, mustard, salt, sugar, and mayonnaise. Add to cooked macaroni, onion, celery, and pepper.

Sandra Lee Rufener, St. Paul's United Church of Christ, Mineral City, Ohio

SPAGHETTI SALAD

1—7 oz. box thin spaghetti
3 raw tomatoes, chopped
6 green onions, chopped
(tops also)
2 cucumbers, peeled and chopped

1—8 oz. bottle Zesty Italian
dressing
1/2 bottle McCormick's Salad
Seasoning Supreme

Break spaghetti into 1'' pieces. Cook as directed and rinse in cold water. Add remaining ingredients and mix together.

Should be made a few hours ahead of use. Makes large salad. Keeps well in refrigerator.

Betty J. Warford, Central United Methodist Church, Oblong, Illinois

VEGETABLE SALAD

1 large head cauliflower
1 bunch broccoli
6 stalks celery

1/2–1 lb. carrots
Onion to taste

Cut vegetables in bite-size pieces. Toss with dressing.

DRESSING

1-1/2 cups mayonnaise
1 cup sour cream
1 T. lemon juice

1 T. Parmesan cheese
Salt and pepper to taste

Carol Dick, First Lutheran Church of Crystal, Brooklyn Park, Minnesota

BROCCOLI SALAD

2 lbs. fresh broccoli, cut in bite-
    size pieces (stalks and all)

3 large carrots
1/2 large onion

Cut fresh broccoli into bite-size pieces. Peel the carrots and dice into bite-size pieces. Chop onion into small pieces.

DRESSING

1-3/4 cups Hellman's
    mayonnaise
5 oz. cheddar cheese, grated

1 t. garlic powder
2 t. celery salt

Mix the dressing from above and pour onto fresh vegetables. Store in tight container in refrigerator.

Mrs. Marcia Harris, First Christian Church, Muscatine, Iowa

BROCCOLI SALAD

1 bunch fresh broccoli
1 cup mozzarella cheese, grated
1/2 medium purple onion

8 slices bacon, fried crisp and
    crumbled

Wash broccoli; break into pieces. Cut stalk as far as tender. Add other ingredients and mix with dressing.

DRESSING

1/2 cup mayonnaise
1/4 cup sugar

1 T. red wine vinegar

June finds it helpful to heat the vinegar to dissolve the sugar before mixing.

June Hoyland, Pleasant Hill Church of The Brethren, Johnstown, Pennsylvania

SKAGIT VALLEY SALAD

1 head cauliflower, break into
    small pieces
3 stalks broccoli, break into
    small pieces
1 bunch green onions, chopped
1 cup mayonnaise

1/2 cup sour cream
1 T. granulated sugar
1 T. white vinegar
Dash of Worcestershire sauce
Dash of Tabasco sauce
Salt to taste

Mix vegetables together. Mix remaining ingredients together until smooth. Pour salad dressing mixture over vegetables and stir. Refrigerate for a couple hours before serving.

Mike Yeoman, First Baptist Church, Mount Vernon, Washington

MARINATED GREEN BEANS

2 cans cut beans, drained
1 onion, sliced thin
1 clove garlic
2 T. sugar
1 T. paprika
1/4 t. salt

2 T. chopped parsley
1 t. oregano
1 t. prepared dry mustard
1/3 cup vinegar
1/4 cup salad oil

Mix all ingredients. Marinate 4–6 hours. Take out garlic pod.
This recipe will keep for weeks. You may add beans once more.

Emmie Mayhand, St. Thomas Episcopal Church, Columbus, Georgia

MEXICAN SALAD

1 head lettuce
2–3 tomatoes
1 cup sharp cheese
1 bottle Catalina salad dressing

1 small bunch fresh onions
1 can ranch style beans, drained
1 small bag Fritos

Mix all together. Add Fritos right before serving so they will be crisp.
Small amount of hamburger meat, cooked, seasoned, and drained may
be added if desired.

Mrs. Delores Gautier, Memorial Baptist Church, Killeen, Texas

HOT CHINESE STYLE SLAW

1/2 large head cabbage, cut in
   2'' squares, rinsed and
   drained
4 cups boiling water

Salt to taste
1–1-1/2 t. crushed red pepper
4 cloves garlic, crushed

Pack cabbage in 2-quart jar or container with tight-fitting lid. Add
remaining ingredients. Cover tight; let stand at room temperature for
24 hours. Will keep refrigerated up to 2 weeks. Makes 10 servings
and the liquid may be reused.

Dave Copley, Fairview Baptist Church, Statesville, North Carolina

FREEZER COLE SLAW

8 cups cabbage, shredded
1 carrot, shredded
1 pepper, diced fine
2 t. salt

1 cup vinegar
2 cups sugar
1 t. celery seed
1 t. mustard seed

Mix first 4 ingredients together and let set 1 hour. Squeeze or press water out. Heat to boiling the vinegar, sugar, celery seed, and mustard seed. Pour hot on cabbage. Stir well, cool, and freeze. This will also keep for several weeks in the refrigerator.

This is excellent for freezing when cabbage is in season and can also be made ahead to take to a potluck.

Mary Jane Miller, Emmaus Lutheran Church, Wauseon, Ohio

CHURCH COLE SLAW

This recipe has been used by the ladies of First United Methodist for several years.

2 qts. cabbage, shredded
1 green pepper
1 red pepper
4 t. salt
2 cups water
2 cups sugar

1 cup water
1 cup vinegar
4 t. mustard seed
4 t. celery seed
4 stalks celery

Mix first 5 ingredients together and let stand 2 hours. Do not drain. Cut celery fine. Add all remaining ingredients to cabbage mixture. Let stand overnight. Makes two large dishes and keeps several days.

Lonne Kay Mackie, First United Methodist Church, Blair, Nebraska

SPINACH SALAD

Equal parts of spinach and
    lettuce

Hard boiled eggs
Little green onions

Add dressing and garnish with hard boiled eggs and pimientos. Do not refrigerate; let stand at room temperature.

DRESSING

1 pt. salad dressing
1/2 lb. bacon, diced and fried crisp

3 T. bacon fat

Mix all ingredients together and pour over top.

Rev. Paul W. Bowles, The Ossining United Methodist Church, Ossining, New York

SPINACH AND MUSHROOM SALAD

1-1/2 lb. fresh spinach
1/2 lb. fresh mushrooms
1/2 cup vegetable oil
3 t. white wine vinegar
1 T. onion, grated

2 t. Dijon mustard
1 t. salt
1 t. sugar
4 slices bacon, cooked and
 crumbled

Wash, stem, and break spinach. Wash mushrooms and slice. For dressing, mix oil, vinegar, onion, mustard, salt, and sugar until the sugar is well dissolved. Mix together with other ingredients except bacon. Toss until well coated. Sprinkle with bacon and serve immediately. Serves 8–10.

Dressing can be made ahead and reserved until serving.

Betty Metts, East Frankfort Baptist Church, Frankfort, Kentucky

ZUCCHINI SALAD

3 medium size very fresh
 zucchini, thinly sliced
2/3 cup cider vinegar
1/2 cup bell pepper, shredded
1/2 cup celery, shredded
1/2 cup yellow onion, shredded

1/2 cup sugar
1/3 cup oil
2 T. red wine vinegar
1 t. salt
1/2 t. pepper, freshly ground

Combine all ingredients thoroughly. Cover and refrigerate at least 6 hours before serving. Serves 6 and will keep 2 weeks in refrigerator.

Fran Sharp, Main Street United Methodist Church, Hattiesburg, Mississippi

TEN HOUR LAYER SALAD

1 head lettuce, torn apart
1 cup celery, diced
6 hard boiled eggs, diced
10 oz. frozen peas, thawed
1/2 cup green pepper, chopped
1/2 cup cucumber, diced
1-1/2 cups carrots, grated

10 slices bacon, fried and cut up
1 medium onion, diced
2 cups mayonnaise sweetened
 with 2 T. sugar
2 cups cheddar cheese, grated
6 small tomatoes, cut up

Use 9''x12'' pan. Put vegetables in layers as listed up to and including the onion. Spread the mayonnaise over the salad as if frosting a cake. Place grated cheese on top. Prepare 10 hours in advance or day before; refrigerate. Before serving, garnish with tomatoes. Serve salad as it has been prepared without tossing it.

Judy Ross, Miramar Church of God, Miramar, Florida

HOT TURKEY OR CHICKEN SALAD

2 cups *cooked* chicken, cubed
  (about 2 large breasts)
2 cups celery, diced
1/2 t. salt

2 t. onion, grated
1/2 cup whole almonds
1 cup mayonnaise
2 T. lemon juice

Combine the above and pile lightly in a greased baking dish. Top with 1 cup crushed potato chips, and 1/2 cup grated American cheese. Bake in a 450°F. oven for about 10 minutes.

Kay Neeb, First United Methodist Church, Bad Axe, Michigan

DRESSINGS

SWEET-SOUR SALAD DRESSING

For coleslaw and other salads.

1 small onion
1 cup sugar
1 cup cooking oil
1 t. dry mustard
1 t. salt or seasoned salt

1/2 cup vinegar (may use
  1/4 cup wine vinegar and
  1/4 cup regular vinegar)
1 t. celery seed

Chop small onion in blender. Add sugar, cooking oil, dry mustard, and salt (may use seasoned salt). Mix and blend in blender for 10 minutes. Add vinegar; beat in blender again. Add celery seed; mix again.

Mary C. Adams, Free Hope Baptist Church, Chatsworth, Georgia

CELERY SEED SALAD DRESSING

1-1/4 cups sugar
2 t. dry mustard
2 t. celery seed
2 T. onion, chopped

1/2 t. garlic powder
2 cups cooking oil
1 cup vinegar

Blend in blender for 5 minutes at high speed.

Sandra Lee Rufener, St. Paul's United Church of Christ, Mineral City, Ohio

ANCHOVY SALAD DRESSING

2 eggs
1 can anchovies with oil
1—4 oz. jar artichoke hearts
1 T. green onion tops, chopped
1 clove garlic
1 t. pepper corns

1 T. horseradish mustard
1 pkg. Good Seasons Italian
   dressing (dry)
1 cup salad oil
1/2 cup olive oil

Combine all ingredients in blender, except oils. Blend at high speed. Gradually add in small amounts of oil as it mixes to make a thick mayonnaise. Add oils until all is blended. Store in cold place, covered; will keep 1 week.

Dennis Rutledge, Ozark Lakes Area, Mid-America Christian Church (Disciples), Springfield, Missouri

RICHMOND MUSTARD DRESSING

2 cups cooking oil
1-1/2 cups sugar
1 t. salt
1 T. dry mustard

2 T. onion juice
1 cup cider vinegar
3 T. mustard

Blend in blender until thoroughly blended. Taste of dressing will depend on vinegar and/or mustard used. Refrigerate before serving.

Barry H. Cornwal, Centenary United Methodist Church, Shady Side, Maryland

SALAD DRESSING

1 can tomato soup
1/2 cup sugar
1/2 cup white vinegar
3/4 cup cooking oil
1 t. paprika

1 t. black pepper
1 T. mustard
1 T. salt (1/2 garlic salt and
   1/2 table salt)
1 medium onion, grated

Place all of above ingredients in quart jar and mix well. Refrigerate. This dressing is better if made the day before using.

Mrs. Blair M. Young, Broad Street United Methodist Church, Portsmouth, Virginia

Beef, Pork
and
Lamb

BEEF

LAZY TEXAS BRISKET

1 large garlic clove, minced
1—5 lb. beef brisket
1 T. chili powder
1 t. paprika
1 t. salt

1/2 t. dried sage
1/2 t. ground cumin
1/4 t. pepper, freshly ground
1/2 t. sugar
1/2 t. oregano

Preheat oven to 225 °F. Rub garlic into both sides of brisket. Combine remaining ingredients and mix well. Rub all into brisket. Set brisket fat side up on large piece of foil and wrap tightly. Put in shallow roasting pan. Bake until tender, about 7–8 hours. Serve hot or cold with sauce.

SAUCE FOR BRISKET

1 stick butter
1 medium onion, chopped
1/2 cup water
1/2 cup chili sauce
1/2 cup ketchup
1/4 cup vinegar
2 T. brown sugar

2 T. lemon juice
2 T. Worcestershire sauce
1 T. molasses
2 t. salt
2 t. dried mustard
1/2 t. pepper, freshly ground
1/2 t. paprika

Fry onion in butter until transparent. Blend in remaining ingredients. Bring to boil, reduce heat and simmer 30 minutes. Serve at room temperature.

Marie Mourtsen, Maplewood United Methodist Church, Omaha, Nebraska

RUMP ROAST SAUERBRATEN STYLE

3–4 lbs. rump roast
2 T. cooking oil
2 t. salt
1/4 t. pepper
1/2 cup grape jelly
3 medium onions, sliced

1/2 cup wine vinegar
1/3 cup water
1 t. kitchen bouquet
1/2 t. ground ginger
2 bay leaves
1/3 cup flour

Brown meat in oil. Season with salt and pepper. Spread jelly over meat, top with onions. Combine vinegar, water, bouquet, ginger, and leaves. Pour over meat. Cover, cook at low heat 3–3-1/2 hours, basting. Discard bay leaves. Add flour, make gravy.

Mrs. Gerald Schuster, Bayport United Methodist Church, Bayport, Long Island, New York

STIR-FRY PEPPER STEAK

1 T. oil
1 medium green pepper,
   sliced thin
1/2 lb. boneless sirloin steak
   (thin strips)
1—8 oz. can sliced water
   chestnuts, drained

1 envelope instant onion
   soup mix
2 t. brown sugar
1 t. cornstarch
1/4 t. ground ginger
1/2 cup water
Hot cooked rice

In large skillet or wok, heat oil and cook green pepper 1 minute. Add beef and cook 2 minutes, stirring frequently. Add water chestnuts and instant onion soup mix, sugar, cornstarch, and ginger blended with water. Stirring frequently, cook 1 minute or until sauce is thickened. Serve with hot rice and soy sauce, if desired. Serves 2.

Karen Mozingo, Wesley Chapel United Methodist Church, Lydia, South Carolina

CHICAGO ITALIAN BEEF

1—12 lb. rump roast
5 large onions

1 whole head garlic, peeled
1 large green pepper

Combine onions, garlic, and green pepper in blender until it looks like a paste. Put paste over rump roast. Salt and pepper to taste. Roast at 325°F. 30–40 minutes per pound. Basil and oregano may be added. While roasting, add hot water to sides of pan to cover one-third of meat. Roast uncovered. Add beef bouillon cubes to water for stronger taste to juice. Slice meat as thin as possible and serve with juice on sliced French bread.

Deborah Plimmer, Eastern Heights Church, Cleburne, Texas

BEEFSTEAK PIE

1-1/2 cups onions, sliced
1/3 cup cooking oil
1-1/2 lbs. round steak, cut into
   1/2" pieces
1/3 cup flour
2 t. all-purpose seasoning

1/4 t. black pepper
3-1/4 cups boiling water
1 T. Worcestershire sauce
1 cup raw potatoes, cut into
   1/2" cubes
Pie crusts to cover pie

Fry onions slowly in hot oil until soft; remove and save. Roll meat in mixture of flour and seasoning; brown in hot oil. Add boiling water and Worcestershire sauce. Sprinkle in any remaining flour. Cover, simmer until meat is tender (about 1 hour). Add potatoes, cook 10 minutes longer. Pour into baking pan. Place onions on top; cover with pastry. Bake in a 450°F. oven for 30 minutes.

Sibyl Bryan, Bethany Baptist Church, Snellville, Georgia

FAKE FILETS

1 lb. ground beef
2 T. onion, chopped
1 egg, beaten
1/2 cup cheese

1-1/2 T. ketchup
1-1/2 T. Lea and Perrins sauce
1/2 t. salt
Bacon strips

Mix thoroughly. Shape meat mixture into filets and wrap bacon around them; stick with toothpick to hold. Broil each side 5 minutes.

Martina (Marty) Wohkittel, Covenant Presbyterian Church, Carrollton, Texas

ROUND STEAK

2 lbs. round steak
2/3 cup water
1 pkg. dry onion soup mix
1—2 oz. can mushrooms

1 cup sour cream
2 T. flour
Oil or shortening

Trim steak and cut into strips. Brown in oil or shortening. Add water, soup mix, mushrooms, sour cream, and flour. Cover and simmer until tender. Or bake at 350°F. until tender.

Eleanor says this recipe was given to her by her sister Jan, and it is delicious!

Mrs. Eleanor M. Tweito, Redeemer Lutheran Church, Marshall, Missouri

OVEN STROGANOFF

2-1/2 lbs. round or chuck steak,
    cut into bite-sized pieces
1 can cream of mushroom
    soup, undiluted
1 can cream of celery
    soup, undiluted

1 can French onion soup,
    undiluted
4 oz. sour cream (more if
    desired)
Noodles or rice to serve 4–6

Place pieces of steak in a small roaster. Pour the soups over the meat. Cover and bake at 250°F. 5–6 hours. Gently stir some of gravy into sour cream. Add sour cream mixture to the rest of the stroganoff. Serve over noodles or rice.

This recipe doubles or triples easily. Also, extra onions may be added at the beginning of the cooking for extra flavor. Shirley also adds fresh mushrooms during the last hour for a special touch.

Mrs. Shirley Meade, First Assembly of God, Crestview, Florida

ORIENTAL STEAK DINNER

2 lbs. round steak, thin slices
1/2 cup soy sauce
1/4 cup water
1/4 cup garlic powder
1/4 cup salad oil (omit if you
    use a non-stick skillet)
1—15 oz. can fancy mixed Chinese vegetables

1—16 oz. pkg. frozen San
    Francisco blend vegetables
    (or other suitable
    combinations)
2 T. cornstarch
2 cups water

Combine soy sauce, water, and garlic powder. Marinate sliced beef in this mixture for 15 minutes. Drain meat, keeping liquid mixture. Brown meat quickly, then let simmer about 15 minutes. Add two containers of vegetables. Cook slowly another 10–15 minutes. Combine cornstarch with water. Add marinate liquid. Pour over meat and vegetable mixture. Continue to cook until somewhat thick and blended. Serve over rice or Chinese noodles.

Marilyn J. Richardson, Muncie District Office United Methodist Church, Muncie, Indiana

HUNGARIAN GOULASH

A family recipe for 4 generations, originating in Hungary.

2 lbs. beef
1 large onion
1 clove garlic
1 T. paprika

1 T. shortening
1 t. dill (or Accent)
1/2 sharp pepper
1/2 cup water

Cut onion, garlic, and pepper into small cubes. Add to shortening, along with dill (or Accent) and water. Season to taste. Simmer 15 minutes. Cut beef into cubes, add to the simmered mixture. Continue simmering 1-1/2–2 hours or until tender. Serve with buttered noodles.

Mrs. Lester Stock, Pilgrim Evangelical Lutheran Church, Wauwatosa, Wisconsin

UNUSUAL MEATLOAF

1-1/2 lbs. ground beef
1/2 small onion, chopped
1 t. Worcestershire sauce
1 t. soy sauce

1/2 cup ketchup
1 egg
1 T. grape jelly

Mix all the ingredients together and cover. Set in refrigerator overnight to allow flavors to blend. Next day add enough cracker crumbs to make firm. Form into loaf and bake at 350°F. for 45 minutes.

Debbie Bell, Suncoast Christian Church, Bradenton, Florida

LIVER CREOLE

For non-liver-lovers, like kids!

2 lbs. calf liver, washed and
  drained
Adolph's meat tenderizer
  (optional)
1/2 stick margarine

1—8 oz. can tomato sauce
1 medium onion, chopped
1/2 cup flour
1 bell pepper, diced
Salt and pepper to taste

Sprinkle meat tenderizer over meat. Melt margarine in skillet over medium burner. Roll each piece of meat in flour and braise on both sides in skillet. When browned, remove liver to platter and add onion, bell pepper, and remaining flour to skillet. Replace liver in skillet. Pour tomato sauce evenly over liver. Put lid on skillet and simmer about 20 minutes or until done. Serves 4.

Zuetta Putty, Eastern Heights Church, Cleburne, Texas

AUNT SOPHIE'S SWEDISH MEATBALLS

Great for potlucks and picnics served in a crock pot.

1 lb. hamburger
1 egg
1/2 cup bread crumbs
2 T. onions, chopped

2 T. dill pickles, chopped
Little bit of milk
1 can mushroom soup,
  undiluted

Mix all ingredients except soup. Brown meatballs. Remove extra grease from browning. Pour soup in skillet with meatballs. Simmer 1/2–1 hour. This recipe can be doubled.

Sandy Hunter, Saegertown United Methodist Church, Saegertown, Pennsylvania

SPANISH RICE CASSEROLE

1 lb. ground beef
1 can tomato soup
1 can tomato sauce
1 small jar mushrooms

1/4 cup onions
1 cup Minute Rice, cooked
1 large pkg. mozzarella cheese

Brown hamburger meat and onions together. Cook rice while browning ground beef. Drain grease from meat. Add tomato soup, tomato sauce, and mushrooms. Mix well and add rice. Combine well. Pour half of the mixture into a large casserole dish. Sprinkle with half the pack of cheese. Pour remaining mixture in dish and top with remaining cheese. Cook in preheated 350°F. oven for 20–30 minutes or until cheese is melted and bubbly.

Deborah Ray, First Free Will Baptist Church, Columbus, Mississippi

GROUND BEEF AND WILD RICE CASSEROLE

1 pkg. wild and brown rice	1 can water
2 T. onion, chopped	1 lb. ground beef
1 can mushroom soup	1 cup celery, chopped
1 can cream of chicken soup	3 T. soy sauce

Prepare rice according to directions on box. Brown meat; add onion, celery, and soy sauce. Stir in soups and water; mix thoroughly. Add rice mixture. Bake in shallow pan at 375 °F. for 30–40 minutes, uncovered.

Marquita Butcher, First Baptist Church, Rogers, Arkansas

FIVE-LAYER CASSEROLE DISH

4 potatoes	1/2–2/3 cup tomato juice
3 onions	Salt
1 lb. hamburger	Pepper
1—#2 can tomatoes	1 deep casserole, buttered
2/3 cup regular rice, *not* instant	

Slice potatoes to 1/8'' thickness. Slice onions to same thickness. Layer potatoes; seasoning; onions; hamburger; seasoning. Pour tomatoes over hamburger. Layer rice on top of tomatoes. Pour tomato juice over and run knife through so that it gets through to bottom. Bake at 325 °F. for 2-1/2–3 hours, or you can cook longer at a lower temperature.

This makes a good full meal dish if you plan to be gone for several hours.

Mrs. Wayne Sneller, Central Christian Church, Decatur, Illinois

CAJUN RICE DRESSING

1 lb. hamburger meat	1 can cream of chicken soup
3/4 cup celery, chopped	1 can cream of onion soup
3/4 cup bell pepper, chopped	2 cups raw rice ·
3/4 cup onion, chopped	2 cups water
3/4 cup parsley, chopped	Season to taste
2 cloves garlic, minced	

Brown hamburger meat and mix with all remaining ingredients. Bake at 350 °F. in a tightly covered casserole dish for approximately one hour.

Monica Neel, First Assembly of God, New Iberia, Louisiana

DAIRY DISH

This is a favorite potluck dish including many dairy items produced in this "Dairyland."

1/2 lb. egg noodles	1—8 oz. can tomato sauce
1 lb. ground beef	1 cup creamed cottage cheese
1 T. butter	1 cup sour cream
1 t. salt	6 green onions, chopped
1/4 t. garlic salt	3/4 cup cheddar cheese,
1/8 t. pepper	shredded

Cook noodles, rinse and drain. Brown beef in butter. Add salt, garlic, pepper, and tomato sauce. Simmer 5 minutes. Mix noodles, cottage cheese, sour cream, and onions. Mix together with sauce/meat mixture. Top with shredded cheese. Bake at 350°F. for 20 minutes, or until cheese has melted and browned. Makes 8 servings.

Julaine Raduechel, First Presbyterian Church, Wausau, Wisconsin

BEEF ROLLS DELUXE

1-1/2 lbs. ground beef	2 T. Parmesan cheese
1/2 fine bread crumbs or	1/2 cup tomato juice
cracker crumbs	Salt and pepper to taste
1 egg	

Mix together and form into 12 rolls. Wrap each roll in a cooked lasagna noodle (cooked according to directions on package and cut in half crosswise). Place in buttered baking dish and pour sauce for meat rolls over rolls. Bake in a 350°F. oven for approximately 1 hour. Uncover and sprinkle 6 ounces shredded mozzarella cheese over top. Bake an additional 5 minutes or until cheese is melted.

SAUCE

3 T. salad oil	1 t. basil
1 medium onion, chopped	2 cups tomato juice
1 small can tomato paste	Salt, pepper, and garlic to taste
1 t. oregano or Italian seasoning	

Cook onion in oil until light brown. Add rest of ingredients and simmer 8–10 minutes. If this makes too much for one meal, the remainder, rolls and all, may be frozen.

Janet Thatcher, Sunbury Church of Christ, Sunbury, Ohio

BAKED BEAN CASSEROLE

1 lb. ground chuck
2 cans pork and beans
1 medium onion
1 green pepper

1/2 cup chili sauce
1 T. mustard
1/2 cup brown sugar

Brown meat. Drain off fat. Combine remainder of ingredients. Cover and bake at 400°F. for 30 minutes.

Gloria Burch, Green Valley Church of God, St. Albans, Wyoming

POTATO PIZZA

1 can cheddar cheese soup
1/2 cup milk

1 lb. hamburger, browned
6 cups potatoes, thinly sliced

Mix well, put in 9''x13'' pan. Over top put 1 small can tomato sauce, 1/2 cup chopped onion, oregano, and pepper. Dot with butter, cover with foil. Bake at 375°F. for 2 hours or more. Serve with Parmesan or mozzarella cheese.

Virginia E. Grems, Christian Church, Estherville, Iowa

PIZZA CASSEROLE

2—10-1/2 oz. cans pizza sauce
with cheese
2 small or 1—14 oz. can
tomato sauce
2 lbs. ground beef

1 medium onion
2 cups noodles
2 cups sharp cheddar cheese
2 cups mozzarella cheese

Mix and brown hamburger and onion. Add pizza sauce and tomato sauce. Cook noodles approximately 3 minutes. Grease a 9''x13'' cake pan with butter and pour half of mixture in pan. Sprinkle half of the cheese, then mixture and then cheese again. Bake at 400°F. for 45 minutes or until cheese browns. Delicious!

Darlene Walters, Eaton Road Nazarene Church, Hamilton, Ohio

SPAGHETTI PIE

Served at an Appreciation Dinner for the Vacation Bible School staff.

6 oz. spaghetti, uncooked
2 T. butter or margarine
1/3 cup Parmesan cheese, grated
2 eggs, well-beaten
1 lb. ground beef or bulk pork sausage
1/2 cup onion, chopped
1/4 cup green pepper, chopped

1—8 oz. can (1 cup) tomatoes, cut up
1—6 oz. can tomato paste
1 t. sugar
1 t. dried oregano, crushed
1/2 t. garlic salt
1 cup (8 oz.) cottage cheese
1/2 cup (2 oz.) mozzarella cheese, shredded

Cook the spaghetti according to package directions; drain (should have about 3-1/4 cups spaghetti). Stir butter or margarine into hot spaghetti. Stir in Parmesan cheese and eggs. Form spaghetti mixture into crust in a buttered 10'' pie plate.

In skillet, cook ground beef or pork sausage, onion, and green pepper until vegetables are tender and meat is browned. Drain off excess fat. Stir in undrained tomatoes, tomato paste, sugar, oregano, and garlic salt. Heat through.

Spread cottage cheese over bottom of spaghetti crust. Fill pie with tomato mixture. Bake, uncovered, in 350°F. oven for 20 minutes. Sprinkle the mozzarella cheese atop. Bake 5 minutes longer or until cheese melts. Makes 6 servings.

Mrs. Dolores Kratz, Plains Mennonite Church, Lansdale, Pennsylvania

QUICK AND EASY PIZZA SPAGHETTI

1 stick pepperoni
1—15 oz. can tomato sauce
1 small onion

1 lb. mozzarella cheese, grated
1 lb. spaghetti
Seasonings to taste

Slice the pepperoni and brown with the chopped onion in a saucepan. Add the tomato sauce and seasonings; heat through while the spaghetti is cooking. Drain and rinse the spaghetti and put in serving bowl. Sprinkle the cheese on top of spaghetti and pour the sauce over all. Mix together. Enjoy!

Sally Kiewicz, Redemption Lutheran Church, Detroit, Michigan

DONNA'S ITALIAN SPAGHETTI

2 lbs. ground meat
2—28 oz. cans tomatoes
2—4 oz. cans tomato paste
2 cloves garlic or garlic powder
   to taste
1–2 bay leaves

1/4–1/2 t. dried oregano or
   to taste
Salt and pepper
1/4 t. dried red peppers,
   crushed

Chop tomatoes in large chunks, removing any hard cores; place tomatoes and juice in large heavy kettle or 5-quart Dutch oven. Add tomato paste and spices. Add 1-1/2 cans of water. Mix well and place over medium burner. Bring to boil, lower heat to keep sauce on gentle boil. Brown ground meat. Drain well. Add to sauce mixture. Continue to boil gently until sauce is thick and about half of original volume.

To really make the sauce delicious, midway through the cooking (2 hours) add 8 ounces of thinly sliced pepperoni. Usual length of cooking time is three to four hours. Ladle sauce over individual servings and serve with tossed salad, bread sticks, hard rolls or garlic bread.

Tip on cooking spaghetti: Bring water to boil, salt, add spaghetti, bring to a boil again. Turn off burner, put lid on kettle and let set for 20 minutes for perfect spaghetti every time.

Donna Byrum, First Baptist Church-Robinson, Waco, Texas

POOR BOY'S LASAGNE

1 lb. ground beef
2 cans tomato sauce
3 T. onion, chopped
1—8 oz. pkg. cream cheese

1 cup cottage cheese
1/4 pt. sour cream
1 pkg. lasagne noodles
Parmesan cheese

Brown meat. Add tomato sauce and set aside. Mix cheese, onions, and sour cream at room temperature. Cook noodles according to directions on package. Butter casserole dish. Place layer of noodles on bottom of casserole; then the cheese, and another layer of noodles. Top with tomato and meat sauce. Pack down and chill 2–3 hours. Top with Parmesan cheese. Bake at 350°F. for 35–40 minutes.

Can be made the day before and stored in refrigerator until ready to bake. It can also be frozen, then baked. Delicious and easy to make for potlucks, etc.

Shelley Burnett, Community Christian Church, San Juan Capistrano, California

QUICK CRESCENT TACO PIE

1–1-1/4 lbs. ground beef
1—1-1/4 oz. pkg. taco or chili
   seasoning mix*
1/2 cup water
1/3 cup stuffed green olives or
   pitted ripe olives, sliced
1—8 oz. can Pillsbury
   Refrigerated Quick Crescent
   Dinner Rolls

1-1/2–2 cups corn chips,
   crushed
1 cup (8 oz. or 1/2 pt.) dairy
   sour cream
6 slices American cheese or
   1 cup (4 oz.) cheddar cheese,
   shredded
Shredded lettuce, if desired
Avocado slices, if desired

In large fry pan, brown ground beef; drain. Stir in seasoning mix, water, and olives; simmer 5 minutes. Meanwhile, separate crescent dough into 8 triangles. Place triangles in ungreased 9'' or 10'' pie pan, pressing to form a crust. Sprinkle 1 cup corn chips over bottom of crust. Spoon meat mixture over crust and corn chips. Spread sour cream over meat mixture; cover with cheese. Sprinkle on remaining corn chips. Bake at 375°F. for 20–25 minutes until crust is golden brown. If desired, serve in wedges topped with shredded lettuce and avocado slices. Yield: 4–6 servings.

*Tip: Mixture of 1/4 cup ketchup, 1–2 T. chili powder, 1 T. instant minced onion, 1/2 t. minced garlic, and 1/4 t. Tabasco sauce can be used for taco seasoning mix. Or 1/2 cup taco sauce can be used for taco seasoning mix and water.

Ann Bouknight, Holy Cross Lutheran Church, Springfield, New Jersey

EASY STROMBOLI

1 loaf frozen bread dough
8 oz. cheese, grated (cheddar or
   mozzarella, your choice)
1—4 oz. can mushrooms
Green pepper (optional)
Onions (optional)
1 small jar spaghetti sauce

Combination of any 2 of meats:
   1/4 lb. hamburger, browned
     and drained
   1/4 lb. sausage, browned
     and drained
   1/4 lb. cold ham
   1/4 lb. pepperoni
   1/4 lb. salami

Let bread dough rise according to package directions. Roll out dough flat and long (approximately 4''–5'' by 20''–24''). Spread 4 tablespoons spaghetti sauce on bottom, then proceed to fill first with cheese, choice of 2 of the meats listed above, mushrooms, green peppers, onions, etc. Fold over and secure top with toothpicks, if necessary. Place on cookie sheet or foil and rub with oil. Sprinkle with oregano and bake at 425°F. for 15–20 minutes.

M. Darlene Davidson, Newburg United Methodist Church, Newburg, Pennsylvania

TIJUANA PIE

1-1/2 lbs. ground beef
1 onion, chopped
1 clove garlic, minced
1 t. salt
1/4 t. pepper
3/4 lb. cheddar cheese, grated
6 tortillas

1—10 oz. can enchilada sauce
1—8 oz. can tomato sauce
2—16 oz. cans chili seasoned
beans
1—16 oz. can corn, drained
1—6 oz. can green olives
1—6 oz. can black olives

Brown beef, onion, and garlic in skillet. Pour off excess fat and season with salt and pepper. Wipe inside of 4-quart crock pot with oil. Place tortilla in bottom of pot; spoon some meat mix on it. Add a little sauce and cheese. Top with another tortilla and layer on bean, cheese, and corn section. Drop in a few olives. Continue layers of filling sauce, cheese and olives, finishing off with the cheese and olive top. Cover and cook at low heat for 5–7 hours. Serve with additional hot tortillas. Serves 8–10 people.

NOTE: Tossed salad and garlic bread complete the meal.

Carol A. Wolbaugh, St. Paul's Lutheran Church, Smithville, Ohio

CABBAGE BURGER BAKE

1 small head cabbage, shredded
6 slices bacon
1 medium onion, chopped
1 cup rice, uncooked
1 lb. ground beef
1/2 lb. ground pork

1 t. salt
Pepper
1—15-1/2 oz. can spaghetti
sauce with mushrooms
3 cups water

Spread half of the cabbage in buttered 12-cup baking dish. Saute' bacon until fat starts to cook out; remove, set aside. Stir onion and rice into bacon drippings. Cook until onion is soft and rice lightly browned. Spoon over cabbage. Brown the ground beef and pork mixture in the same pan. Spoon over rice mixture. Add salt and pepper. Top with rest of shredded cabbage. Top with bacon. Heat spaghetti sauce with the water and pour over cabbage. Cover with foil and bake at 400°F. for 50 minutes or until rice and cabbage are tender. Uncover and bake 10 minutes to crisp the bacon.

Inez Roberts, West York Church Of The Brethren, York, Pennsylvania

LEBANESE CABBAGE ROLLS

1 medium cabbage
1-1/2 lbs. ground beef
1 cup rice, cooked
1 egg, lightly beaten
1-1/2 t. salt

1/2 t. pepper
1 lb. 4 oz. can tomato juice
1 t. ginger
1 t. cinnamon

Put cabbage in mixing bowl, cover with boiling salted water. Let stand for 10 minutes, drain, cut out core of cabbage. Separate leaves. If they do not come off easily, return cabbage to boiling water for a few minutes. Trim down thick edge on back of leaves to make them easier to roll.

Prepare filling: Combine beef, rice, egg, salt, and pepper. Mix well. Place mixture in center of each cabbage leaf. Roll up leaves like a jelly roll, folding in sides of leaves to seal filling completely. Place rolls in large skillet, add tomato juice. Cover; simmer 1-1/2 hours.

Mrs. Peggye McNeill, Reinhardt Bible Church, Dallas, Texas

EGG ROLLS

1 lb. ground beef or pork
1/2 head cabbage, shredded
6 green onions (include tops), chopped
1/2 cup bean sprouts, drained (canned or fresh)

1/2 cup water chestnuts, drained and chopped
1/2 cup celery, chopped

Brown meat in skillet in slight amount of hot oil. Remove meat. Add cabbage and onion to drippings, stir until transparent or limp. Add bean sprouts and water chestnuts. Season as desired with Accent, pepper, 1/2 teaspoon sugar, some grated ginger root, garlic, 1 teaspoon soy sauce; salt to taste. Vegetables should be slightly crisp. Add meat (off fire). Stir all and cool to room temperature. Fill and roll skins tight according to directions on package; fry in hot oil.

The filling can be adjusted to your family's tastes, both ingredients and proportion used. This amount will fill more than 1 package of skins. Leftover filling is good in pita bread or just as a sandwich.

Carolyn Clubine, First United Methodist Church, Dunkerton, Iowa

REUBEN CASSEROLE

1 lb. 11 oz. can sauerkraut, drained
2 medium tomatoes, diced
2 T. thousand island dressing
2 T. butter
2 cups Swiss cheese, shredded
1 can flaky buttermilk biscuits
2 Krispy Rye crackers, crushed
1/2 t. caraway seeds

2—4 oz. pkgs. sliced corned beef or shredded from deli

Spread sauerkraut in 12''x8'' baking dish. Top with tomatoes, dot with butter and dressing. Cover with the corned beef and sprinkle on cheese. Bake at 425°F. for 20 minutes. Remove from oven. Separate each biscuit and place in three rows. Slightly overlap biscuits to form the three rows. Sprinkle with the rye cracker crumbs and caraway seed. Bake at 425°F. for 15–20 minutes or until biscuits are browned. Delicious!

Ruth Blattner, First Presbyterian Church, Murrysville, Pennsylvania

CORNED BEEF HOT DISH

12 oz. wide noodles, cooked and drained
1 can corned beef, cut up
1 cup processed cheese (American or Velveeta), cubed
2 cans cream of chicken soup
2 soup cans of milk
1/4 cup onion, chopped
1—12 oz. bag potato chips, crushed

Mix all ingredients, reserving half the potato chips. Bake at 300°F. for 1 hour. Sprinkle remaining potato chips on top and bake an additional 10 minutes. Serves 8.

A favorite dish which can be easily expanded to make any amount needed to serve a few or many.

Julaine Raduechel, First Presbyterian Church, Wausau, Wisconsin

PORK

SUNDAY BAKED PORK CHOPS

4–6 pork chops
Salt
1 can cream of chicken soup

3 T. ketchup
1 T. Worcestershire sauce

Arrange chops in shallow pan and add salt to taste. Combine other ingredients and spread over the chops. Bake uncovered at 275°F. for 2 hours or at 350°F. for 45 minutes. Use sauce as gravy. Yield: 4–6 servings.

Donna Pryor, Nemaha Christian Church, Nemaha, Nebraska

PORK CHOPS AND STUFFING

4 pork chops
3 cups soft bread cubes
2 T. onions, chopped
1/4 cup butter or margarine, melted

1/4 cup water
1/4 t. poultry seasoning
1 can cream of mushroom soup

Brown chops on both sides in skillet, pour off drippings and arrange in baking dish. Lightly mix rest of ingredients together. Place a mound of stuffing on each chop. Blend cream of mushroom soup with 1/3 cup water. Pour over pork chops and stuffing. Bake at 350°F. until done (about 1 hour).

Mary L. Porath, St. Paul's Lutheran Church, Albion, Michigan

SWEET AND SOUR PORK CHOPS

1 cup carrots, thinly sliced
1/4 cup honey
1 T. soy sauce
1 large can pineapple chunks
1 bell pepper, diced
Salt and pepper to taste

1/2 cup lemon juice
1/2 cup onions, chopped
1 bouillon cube
3 T. cornstarch
2 lbs. pork chops
1/2 stick margarine

Brown pork chops in margarine in saucepan and place in baking dish. Salt and pepper to taste. Drain pineapple and reserve juice. Put carrots, bell pepper, onions, and pineapple on top of pork chops. In saucepan, combine lemon juice, honey, soy sauce, bouillon cube, half of the pineapple juice, and cornstarch. Cook over low heat until thickened. Pour over pork chops, cover dish and bake in oven at 350°F. for approximately 15 minutes.

Jayne Miller, Eastern Heights Church, Cleburne, Texas

PORK CHOPS AND RICE

1 cup rice, uncooked	6–8 pork chops
4 T. water	2 T. drippings from pan
2 onions, sliced	2 cans consomme' of beef broth
Salt and pepper	

Put cup uncooked rice in oblong dish. Sprinkle 4 tablespoons water over rice. Fry pork chops to brown then lay on top of rice. Pour drippings over chops. Slice onions over pork chops. Pour beef consomme' over chops. Salt and pepper to taste. Cover with foil and bake at 375°F. for 1 hour.

Mrs. Cora Savidge, Broad Street United Methodist Church, Portsmouth, Virginia

PORK ORIENTAL

1-1/2 lbs. stewing pork	1—8 oz. can pineapple chunks,
1 onion, sliced	drained and juice reserved
3 T. oil	Soy sauce
1 T. flour	1 chicken bouillon cube
Salt and pepper to taste	1—3-1/2 oz. can pimiento,
1 cup water	drained and sliced
1 green pepper, seeded and sliced	

Cut pork into 1'' pieces. Fry onion in oil until lightly browned; remove from pan. Toss pork in flour, salt, and pepper. Fry until brown. Mix in remaining flour, water, vinegar, onion, green pepper, reserved juice, soy sauce, and bouillon cube. Bring to a boil, stirring. Add seasoning to taste and cover. Simmer for 1-1/2 hours. Add pineapple chunks and pimiento. Cook for 15 minutes longer. Serve with rice. Yield: 4 servings.

Debbie S. Fitz, Church Of The Apostles, United Church of Christ, Waynesboro, Pennsylvania

PIGS IN THE BLANKET

1 lb. ground beef	1—15 oz. can tomato paste or
1 head cabbage	sauce
1 onion	1 can water
1 cup rice, uncooked	Salt and pepper to taste

Place cabbage in hot water to soften. Brown ground beef and onion. Carefully peel leaves from cabbage. Mix meat and onion with rice. Roll in cabbage leaves; tuck in ends or use toothpicks. Place in casserole; pour sauce over pigs. Cover and bake at 350°F. for 1 hour.

Agnes Tilly, Kent Lutheran Church, Kent, Washington

ITALIAN SAUSAGE/SPINACH PIE

1 lb. sweet Italian sausage,
  chopped
6 eggs
2—10 oz. pkgs. frozen chopped
  spinach, thawed and drained
1 lb. mozzarella cheese,
  shredded

2/3 cup ricotta
1 t. salt
1/8 t. pepper
1/8 t. garlic powder
2 crust pie shells
1 T. water

In large skillet over medium heat cook sausage until browned; stir and spoon off extra fat. Reserve 1 egg yolk. In large bowl combine remaining eggs with ingredients, except water. Prepare pastry and add mixture. Add top crust; make center hole and slits. Mix reserved egg yolk and water and brush on top of crust. Bake at 375 °F. for 1 hour 15 minutes. It's best to let it sit a while before serving.

Susan Hounsell, St. John's Episcopal Church, Brooklyn, New York

BARBECUED SPARERIBS

3–4 lbs. spareribs
1 lemon
1 large onion
1 cup ketchup
1/3 cup Worcestershire sauce

1 t. chili powder
1 t. salt
2 dashes Tabasco sauce
1-1/2 cups water

Roast spareribs, meaty side up, in 450 °F. oven for 1/2 hour. Drain excess fat. Cover ribs with slices of lemon and onion. Mix all other ingredients, bring to a boil. Pour over spareribs. Bake at 350 °F. for 1-1/2 hours, basting every 15 minutes. If sauce gets too thick, thin with water.

Cindy Saxman, Tarrytown Baptist Church, Austin, Texas

YAMAZETTI

1 lb. pkg. wide noodles
1/2 lb. yellow brick cheese,
  grated
1-1/2 lbs. ground beef or pork
1 onion, minced

Salt and pepper
1 can condensed milk
1 can tomato soup
1 green pepper, minced

Cook noodles 10 minutes and drain. Brown meat and onion together with salt and pepper. Put in baking dish: 1 layer noodles, 1 layer meat, 1 layer grated cheese, 1 layer minced green pepper. Repeat layers, add condensed milk and tomato soup. Bake at 375–400 °F. for 1 hour.

Lovina Beachy, Amish Mennonite Aid, Plain City, Ohio

BARBECUED SPARERIBS

3–4 lbs. spareribs
1 medium onion, chopped
2 T. bacon fat or butter
1/2 cup water
3 T. vinegar
3/4 cup ketchup

1/2 cup celery, chopped
2 T. sugar
2 t. salt
1 t. prepared mustard
2 T. lemon juice
3 T. Worcestershire sauce

Wipe spareribs with damp cloth. Place in shallow baking pan and bake in moderate oven, 350°F., for 30–40 minutes. Pour off fat.

Saute'onion in the 2 tablespoons bacon fat or butter for 5 minutes and add remaining ingredients. Mix well and simmer 5 minutes. Pour over spareribs and continue baking 1-1/2–2 hours. May be cooked in crock pot (medium heat) 7–8 hours.

Janet Thatcher, Sunbury Church of Christ, Sunbury, Ohio

HAM BALLS

2-1/2 lbs. ground ham
1/2 lb. ground pork
2 cups soft bread crumbs

1 cup evaporated milk
2 eggs

Mix well meat, bread crumbs, milk, and eggs. Shape into approximately fifteen 1/2-cup balls; place in 9''x13'' pan. Pour sauce over meatballs. Bake at 300°F. for 1-1/4 hours.

SAUCE

1 cup light brown sugar
1/2 cup water

1/2 cup vinegar
1/2 t. ground mustard

Combine all ingredients; blend well.

Edith Newberry, First Friends Church, Marion, Indiana

INDIVIDUAL HAM LOAF

1 egg
1 lb. ham loaf mixture
 (1/4 lb. ground pork,
 balance ground ham)

1/3 cup cracker crumbs
3/4 cup milk
1 onion, diced

Mix together and make into 8 small loaves. Cook at 350°F. in oven for 30 minutes. Take from oven and pour off excess juice and put sauce over the loaves (be sure the sauce has been brought to a boil). Place back in oven and cook until well glazed, about 15–25 minutes.

SAUCE FOR HAM LOAF

1/2 cup brown sugar
1/4 cup fruit juice

1/4 t. mustard

Bring above to boil.

Mrs. Joan Bowling, First United Methodist Church, Moline, Illinois

LAMB

LAMB HOTDISH

1 lb. ground lamb
1/4 cup fine bread crumbs
1/4 cup onion, chopped
1 egg, beaten
1 can cream of mushroom soup

1 can tomato soup
2 T. vinegar
2 T. brown sugar
2 t. soy sauce
Dash of pepper

Mix lamb, crumbs, onion, and egg; shape into meatballs. In skillet, brown meatballs; pour off fat. Add remaining ingredients. Cover; cook on low heat about 20 minutes or until well done. Stir now and then.

Serve on a hot biscuit, or hot rice, or as a side dish to complement a baked potato, mashed potatoes, etc. Just a very good dish. You may also substitute hamburger for the meat. Bonnie's family eats a lot of lamb, so lamb is their choice.

Bonnie Wunder, First Presbyterian Church, Lake Park, Iowa

ASSYRIAN STEW

A pastor of Assyrian heritage prepares this feast every year for his church's Foreign Food Fair.

1 leg of lamb
1 medium onion, chopped
8 cups green beans, cut,
    either fresh or frozen
2–3 cloves garlic, pressed
3 large cans stewed tomatoes
1 large green pepper, chopped
2 T. paprika

5 stalks celery, chopped
Salt and pepper to taste

* * * * *

8 cups rice already cooked
16 oz. bag of egg noodles,
    lightly browned in oven
    and then cooked
1 lb. butter

Cover lamb with water. Add seasonings, onion, and garlic. Cook in large pot or electric roaster until lamb is tender. Remove lamb leg, cube, and return meat to roaster. Add remaining ingredients and simmer over low heat for several hours. Meanwhile, bake mixture of precooked rice and noodles divided into two separate pans with 1/2 pound butter in each. Stir rice and noodles every 20 minutes for 1 hour. Serve stew over rice and noodles.

Mrs. Curt Joseph, Highland Park Lutheran Church, Des Moines, Iowa

Poultry, Seafood
and
Meatless Dishes

POULTRY

CHICKEN BAKE

1—2-1/2–3 lb. chicken, cut up   1—16 oz. bottle Russian dressing
1 pkg. Lipton dry onion mix   1—12 oz. jar apricot preserves

Mix ingredients together and pour over chicken in shallow baking dish. Bake at 350°F. for 1-1/2 hours.

Pat Stuckey, First Christian Church, Brazil, Indiana

MICHAEL'S CRANBERRY CHICKEN

1 small whole frying chicken or   1 small onion
   2 Rock Cornish hens   1/2 stick butter or margarine
1 cup cranberry juice   Salt and pepper to taste
1/2 cup cranberry cordial

Season whole bird and brown in butter, rolling frequently. Chop and saute' onions with bird. When brown, add cordial and continue rolling until well coated. Add 1 cup cranberry juice. Cover and simmer until tender. Bird may be halved or quartered.

Michael DeNike, Christ Church, Pompton Lakes, New Jersey

CRISP OVEN-FRIED CHICKEN

1 cup saltine crackers, crushed   1/2 t. onion salt
1/4 cup Parmesan cheese, grated   1/4 t. paprika
1 T. parsley, minced   1/4 t. pepper
1/2 t. salt   2—3 lb. fryers, cut up
1/2 t. oregano leaves   1/2 cup evaporated milk
1/2 t. basil leaves   1/3 cup cooking oil
1/2 t. celery salt

Combine crackers, cheese, parsley, salt, and spices in a bowl. Dip chicken pieces in evaporated milk, then in crumb mixture. Place chicken in shallow baking pan, skin side up. Bake in 375°F. oven for 30 minutes. Brush with oil; continue baking 30 more minutes or until golden brown and tender. Yield: 8 servings.

Microwave: Cook on high 12 minutes, covered with waxed paper. Remove waxed paper, turn dish half a turn, bake uncovered 12–15 minutes on high until done. Will be crisp.

Jackie Mortenson, First Lutheran Church of Crystal, Minneapolis, Minnesota

ROAST CHICKEN WITH VEGETABLES

2—2-2-1/2 lb. broiler fryers, quartered
1 large green pepper, cut in 1'' strips
4 medium potatoes, pared and quartered
1 clove garlic, crushed

1/2 cup cooking or olive oil
1 t. dried oregano leaves
1-1/2 t. salt
1/4 t. pepper
1/4 t. paprika
1—4 oz. can mushroom slices
1 medium onion, sliced

Wipe chicken with damp paper towels. In large shallow baking dish, arrange chicken pieces, green pepper strips, potatoes, mushrooms, and onion slices in a single layer. Preheat oven to 350°F. Combine garlic, oil, and oregano; mix well. Drizzle over chicken and vegetables. Sprinkle all over with salt, pepper, and paprika. Bake uncovered, basting frequently with pan juices, 1 hour or until chicken and potatoes are tender. Increase oven temperature to 400°F. Bake 15 minutes to brown. Arrange chicken with vegetables on warm serving platter, discarding garlic.

If desired, serve with spaghetti with tomato sauce or cheese.

Elaine Diener, St. Mary Church, Louisville, Kentucky

CHICKEN NUGGETS

Chicken (desired amount of skinless, boneless breasts)
Salt
Box of cracker meal

1–2 eggs
10 oz. La Choy sweet and sour sauce

Cut chicken into bite-size pieces, then rinse with cold water. Sprinkle with salt. Refrigerate until ready to cook. Coat pieces with cracker meal, dip into beaten egg (add a little water), then roll in cracker meal again. Fry, drain on paper towel. Serve with sweet and sour sauce.

Linda Batten, Portlock United Methodist Church, Chesapeake, Virginia

BARBECUED CHICKEN FOR WEIGHT WATCHERS

4 chicken breasts, halved
1/4 cup diet cola

1/4 cup ketchup

Skin and remove fat from chicken breasts. Put in a frying pan, flesh side down, and cover with the cola-ketchup mixture. Bring to a fast boil, then cover and lower heat to a simmer. Cook for about 20 minutes, turning once. Remove cover and cook sauce until thickened.

Easy and tasty. The sauce is good over rice, too!

Emmie Mayhand, St. Thomas Episcopal Church, Columbus, Georgia

CHICKEN POT PIE

1 large fryer, stewed and cut up   1 can cream of mushroom soup
in pieces (all white meat may be used)

Stew fryer (or white meat) until done. De-bone and place in 9''x13''
pan. Combine 2 cups chicken broth from stewing and 1 can cream of
mushroom soup. Bring to boil and pour over chicken. Prepare batter
below and dip over chicken by spoonfuls. Bake at 425°F. for 30–40
minutes.

BATTER

1 cup self-rising flour   1 cup buttermilk
1 stick margarine   Pepper to taste

Combine ingredients and mix well.

Mrs. Judy Berry, First Presbyterian Church, Morganton, North Carolina

CHICKEN LOAF

3 lbs. chicken, cooked and diced   1/8 cup pimiento, chopped
2 cups fresh bread crumbs   3 cups chicken broth or
1 cup rice, cooked   mixture of broth and milk
   (measure after cooking)   4 eggs, well beaten
1-1/2 t. salt

Mix all ingredients together, adding eggs last. Bake at 325°F. for 1
hour.

SAUCE

1/4 cup butter or margarine   Optional
1/4 cup flour   1 small can mushrooms
2 cups chicken broth   1/8 t. paprika
1/4 cup milk   2 t. parsley, chopped
1 t. lemon juice
Salt to taste

Melt butter, stir in flour. Add broth, milk, and seasonings as for
gravy; simmer. Makes a light, thin sauce.

Mrs. Cecil Herrin, Gethsemane Baptist Church, Richlands, Virginia

BAKED CHICKEN KIEV

4 whole chicken breasts	1/2 cup Parmesan cheese, grated
4 oz. Monterey Jack cheese	1-1/2 t. oregano
5 T. butter	1/2 t. garlic powder
1 T. parsley	1/4 t. pepper
1/2 cup bread crumbs	4 T. butter

In small bowl mix together: Grated Parmesan cheese, garlic, 1 teaspoon oregano, pepper, and 5 tablespoons melted butter.

In another small bowl mix together: 4 tablespoons melted butter, parsley, and 1/2 teaspoon oregano.

Pound chicken breasts until flat. Spread one side of breasts with butter and cheese mixture. Insert slice of Monterey Jack cheese, then fold like an envelope. Dip breast then into melted butter and parsley mixture. Roll in bread crumbs. Place on flat cookie sheet or jelly roll pan and refrigerate for 4 hours. Bake in 400°F. oven for 20 minutes. Serves 8 and is excellent served with rice pilaf.

Mike Yeoman, First Baptist Church, Mount Vernon, Washington

PARTY CHICKEN

8 large chicken breasts, boned and skin removed	4 oz. chipped beef or boiled ham
8 slices bacon	1 can cream of mushroom soup
	1/2 pt. sour cream

Wrap each chicken breast with a slice of bacon. Line bottom of baking dish (8''x8''x2'') with chipped beef or boiled ham. Arrange chicken breasts on chipped beef or boiled ham. Mix sour cream with soup. Pour over all. Refrigerate. When ready to use, bake at 275°F. for 3 hours, uncovered. Serves 8.

Mrs. Dolores S. Kratz, Plains Mennonite Church, Lansdale, Pennsylvania

BAKED CHICKEN BREASTS

8 boneless chicken breasts	16 slices of bacon
1—8 oz. pkg. Philadelphia cream cheese	1 can cream of chicken soup, undiluted

Cut the cheese into 8 pieces and fold into holes slit in the chicken breasts. Wrap 2 slices of bacon around the breasts and pour the undiluted cream of chicken soup over the chicken. Bake at 350°F. covered for 1 hour, then remove cover and bake 15 minutes more.

Betty Pike, Pleasant Valley Baptist Church, Wichita, Kansas

CREAMY BAKED CHICKEN BREASTS

4 whole chicken breasts, split, skinned and boned
3/4 cup cheddar cheese, shredded
1 cup herb-seasoned stuffing mix
1/4 cup butter or margarine, melted
1—10-3/4 oz. can cream of chicken soup, undiluted

Arrange chicken in a lightly greased 13''x9''x2'' baking dish. Top with cheese. Spread undiluted soup over top and sprinkle with stuffing mix. Drizzle with butter and bake at 350–375°F. for 50–60 minutes. Cover for first 30 minutes. Yield: 8 servings.

Mrs. Donna Cox, Utica United Methodist Church, Sterling Heights, Michigan

TURKEY OR CHICKEN DIVAN

2—10 oz. pkgs. frozen broccoli spears
2 cups sliced turkey or 3 chicken breasts, cooked and boned
2—10-1/2 oz. cans cream of chicken soup
3/4 cup mayonnaise or Miracle Whip
1 t. lemon juice
1 cup cheddar cheese, shredded
1-1/2 cups soft buttered bread crumbs
2 T. butter

Cook broccoli until tender; drain well. Arrange in greased 12''x7''x2'' baking dish. Layer on poultry. Combine undiluted soup, mayonnaise, and lemon juice. Sprinkle with cheese. Top with buttered bread crumbs. Bake at 350°F. about 35 minutes or until heated through. Serves 6–8.

Can use leftover poultry and cut in 1'' chunks.

Lela Patterson, Faith United Methodist Church, North Canton, Ohio

CHICKEN TETRAZZINI

5 T. cooking oil
3 T. flour
1/4 t. salt
1-1/2 cups chicken broth
1—4 oz. can sliced mushrooms
2 cups chopped chicken or turkey
4 oz. spaghetti, cooked
1 cup American cheese, grated
1/2 cup dry bread crumbs

Blend 3 tablespoons cooking oil and flour over medium heat until smooth. Add salt and broth. Cook, stirring until thick. Add mushrooms with liquid. In oiled 2-quart casserole alternate layers of chicken, spaghetti, cheese, and mushroom sauce. Top with crumbs mixed with remaining cooking oil. Bake at 375°F. for 25–30 minutes. Yield: 6 servings

Betty G. Romine, First Baptist Church, Lake Jackson, Texas

SOY CHICKEN

1 cup soy sauce	1 t. ginger
1 cup water	Garlic to taste
1/4 cup sugar or 2 packets of artificial sweetener	

Combine all ingredients and heat. Simmer chicken pieces in mixture in crock pot until done. Then broil or barbecue if desired.

Ruth B. Cawood, Manhattan Baptist Church, Tampa, Florida

BECKY'S CHINESE CHICKEN

1 cup ketchup	1-1/2 T. soy sauce
4 T. brown sugar	1/2 t. ginger
2 T. vinegar	15–16 chicken wings

Mix ingredients until well mixed. Pour sauce over chicken wings and bake at 350°F. for 1-1/2 hours.

Becky Copeland, Bakersfield Church of the Brethren, Bakersfield, California

CASHEW CHICKEN

3 chicken breasts, boned and cut in small pieces	1 small can sliced water chestnuts
1/2 cup green onions, chopped	1 large jar mushroom slices
3 large carrots, sliced	1 small pkg. cashews
2 stalks celery, sliced	1 can chicken broth
1-1/2 cups broccoli, chopped (cauliflower or pea pods could be substituted for broccoli)	1/2 cup water
	1-1/2 T. cornstarch
	1 T. soy sauce
	Dash salt

Put 2 tablespoons oil in electric skillet, place chicken in oil and sauté until nearly done. Remove chicken and reduce heat to simmer. Put broccoli in first then other vegetables and mushrooms. Let simmer for 5–10 minutes then add cashews and chestnuts. When vegetables are done, put chicken back into skillet with vegetables. Add broth, water, cornstarch, and soy sauce. Simmer for about 5–10 minutes.

Serve over wild rice with a green salad or slaw and French bread.

Patsy Blevins, First Free Will Baptist Church, Columbus, Mississippi

CHICKEN A LA KING

1 cup mushrooms, sliced
1/4 cup green pepper,
  chopped finely
1/4 cup margarine
3 T. flour
2 cups half-and-half

1/2 t. salt
1/4 t. pepper
1 egg yolk, beaten
2-1/2 cups cooked chicken
  breasts, diced
2 T. pimiento, finely cut

Lightly brown mushrooms and green pepper in margarine. Add flour, blend. Add half-and-half, salt, and pepper. Cook, stirring constantly. Stir some of the hot mixture into egg yolk and then pour egg into rest of hot mixture. Cook a minute or two, stirring constantly. Add chicken and pimiento. Serve on Pepperidge Farm Pastry Shells (found in frozen food section of store) or over hot biscuits. Makes 6 servings.

Kae Jeffers, First Presbyterian Church, La Junta, Colorado

CHICKEN CACCIATORE

3–4 lb. frying chicken, cut up
2 cups onion rings, thinly sliced
1 medium green pepper,
  chopped
1 clove garlic, crushed
1—1 lb. can tomatoes, partially drained

1—8 oz. can tomato sauce
1—3 oz. can sliced mushrooms,
  drained
1/2 t. salt
1/4–1/2 t. oregano

Place cut up pieces of chicken, skin side up, on foil-lined cookie sheet. Bake in a 350°F. oven for 35–40 minutes. Remove skin and remove chicken from bones. Cook onion rings, green pepper, and garlic in fry pan over medium heat until tender. Stir in remaining ingredients and transfer to Dutch oven. Add chicken pieces to sauce, basting with sauce. Cover tightly and simmer 40 minutes or until thickest pieces are fork-tender. Serve as is or over brown rice. Makes 4 servings.

Elma Yotko, Trinity United Methodist Church, San Antonio, Texas

CHICKEN MEX-I-CAN

4 whole chicken breasts
3 cups water
1 T. salt
1 T. butter
1 medium onion, chopped fine
2 green bell peppers, chopped
   fine
1—1 lb. can tomatoes

1 t. pepper
1/2 t. oregano
1/2 t. salt
1 small can sliced mushrooms
4 T. parsley
1 t. sugar
1 t. chili powder
1 T. cornstarch

Simmer chicken, water, and salt until tender. Cool in broth and remove from bone in large pieces. Set 2 cups of broth aside. Melt butter in skillet. Add onion and green peppers. Stir often until onion is transparent. Add tomatoes, pepper, oregano, salt, mushrooms, parsley, sugar, and chili powder. Add broth. Bring to boil. Mix cornstarch in cold water and add to sauce to thicken. Place chicken in baking dish and pour sauce over the top. Heat in hot oven, 400°F., until bubbly. Serve over mounds of hot buttered rice. Serves 8 people.

Wilma Smith, Riverside Baptist Church, San Antonio, Texas

SOUR CREAM CHICKEN ENCHILADAS

2 whole chicken breasts
2—10-1/2 oz. cans cream of
   chicken soup
1 pt. sour cream
1—4 oz. can chopped green
   chilies (save some for
   garnish)

Ripe olives
Cooking oil
1 dozen corn tortillas
3/4 cup onion, chopped
3 cups grated cheddar or
   Monterey Jack cheese or a
   combination of both

Boil chicken breasts 20–25 minutes. Remove meat from bone and chop. Mix chicken meat, soup, sour cream, and chilies together. Heat oil in small fry pan; dip each tortilla into the hot oil until softened, and drain on paper towels. Spread a thin layer of creamed mixture over the bottom of a 9''x12'' pan. Spread equal amounts of creamed mixture down the middle of each tortilla (reserve some creamed mixture for top) and sprinkle with chopped onion and cheese (reserve some cheese for top). Roll up tortilla and place seam-side down in prepared pan. Pour remaining mixture over the top of rolled tortillas and sprinkle with remaining cheese. Bake at 350°F. for 25–30 minutes. Garnish with black olives and additional chilies. Serves 6–8.

NOTE: This can be prepared ahead of time and refrigerated before baking.

Althea Simpson, Grace Lutheran Church, Vancouver, Washington

SOPA

Mary always brings home an empty dish from potluck dinners with this recipe.

1 medium bag Taco Flavored
    Doritos (Nacho Cheese
    Flavored may be used)
1 can cream of cheddar cheese
    soup

1 can cream of chicken soup
1 small can green chili peppers,
    chopped
1 small can boned chicken
1/2 soup can milk

Place Doritos in casserole dish. Combine other ingredients, pour over Doritos. Poke around with a fork to insure soup mixture gets to most of the Doritos. Bake at 350°F. for 30 minutes or until bubbly. May be microwaved, but reduce milk to 1/4 can.

Mary Hamby, Clay-Platte Baptist Association, Kansas City, Missouri

CHIMICHANGAS DEL PAVO

5 lb. turkey hind half roast
12 oz. green chile salsa
2 t. chili powder
1 t. cumin (comino)
1 t. picante sauce
1 medium onion, chopped

12—8'' flour tortillas
1/2 lb. cheddar cheese, shredded
1/2 lb. Monterey Jack cheese,
    shredded
Lettuce, chopped
Sour cream

Trim turkey roast of excess fat. Cook turkey in crock pot overnight. Remove turkey, let cool. Remove juice from pot. Thicken with flour to make gravy. Return gravy to pot. Add chile salsa, chili powder, cumin, and picante sauce to gravy. Remove meat from bones. Cut or tear meat into bite-size pieces. Return meat to pot. Cook 6—8 hours more. Remove meat and drain.

Warm each tortilla 30 seconds on damp towel in microwave oven. Spoon about 1/4 cup meat and 1 tablespoon onion on tortilla. Roll up like egg roll. Seal edge with small amount of water. Deep fry tortilla until golden brown. Keep in warm oven. To serve: Place chimichangas on plate, spoon gravy over chimichanga. Top with cheese, lettuce, and sour cream.

Ned Daugherty, St. John's Lutheran Church, Fort Collins, Colorado

TURKEY STROGANOFF

1/4 cup green pepper, chopped
2 T. onion, chopped
2 T. butter or margarine
1 can cream of mushroom soup
1/2 cup sour cream

1/4 cup milk
2 cups cooked noodles
1-1/2 cup cooked turkey, diced
1/2 t. paprika

Cook green pepper and onion in butter until tender. In a 2-quart casserole, blend soup, sour cream, and milk. Stir in remaining ingredients. Bake in a 350°F. oven for 35 minutes. Serves 4.

Audrey Peacock, First Methodist Church, Lyons, Georgia

3 CHEESE CHICKEN BAKE

1—8 oz. pkg. wide egg noodles
3 cups cooked chicken, diced
1-1/2 cups cream style cottage
  cheese

2 cups processed American
  cheese, shredded
1/2 cup Parmesan cheese, grated
1 recipe mushroom sauce

Boil noodles until tender and rinse in cold water. Place half the noodles in a buttered pan or casserole. Cover with half of sauce, cottage cheese, chicken, and the other 2 cheeses. Repeat with the noodles and the sauce and 3 cheeses. Bake in a 350°F. oven for 45 minutes. Makes 8 good servings and is great for large luncheons.

MUSHROOM SAUCE

1/2 cup onions, chopped
1/2 cup green peppers, chopped
3 T. butter
1 can condensed cream of
  chicken soup

1/2 cup milk
1—6 oz. can sliced mushrooms
1/4 cup pimiento, chopped
1/2 t. basil

Saute'onions and green peppers in butter. Then stir in rest of ingredients.

Anna Peterson, Ebenezer Lutheran Church, Chicago, Illinois

CREPES ALMONDINE

3 eggs, beaten
2/3 cup flour
1/2 t. salt
1 cup milk
2/3 cup Miracle Whip
3 T. flour
1/2 t. salt
Dash of pepper

1-1/2 cups milk
1 cup Swiss cheese, shredded
2 cups cooked chicken, chopped
1 cup celery, chopped
3/4 cup blanched slivered
  almonds, toasted
1 T. pimiento, chopped
2 T. green onion slices

Combine first 4 ingredients and beat until smooth. Let stand 30 minutes. For each crepe, pour 1/4 cup batter into hot, lightly greased skillet. Cook on one side only.

Combine Miracle Whip, flour, and seasonings. Gradually add milk. Cook, stirring constantly, until thickened. Add cheese, stir until melted. Stir in 1/2 cup almonds and remaining ingredients. Fill each crepe with 1/4 cup chicken mixture, roll up. Place crepes in oblong pan and bake at 350°F. for 20 minutes. Top with remaining sauce and almonds down center. Bake 5 minutes more. Makes 4 servings.

Lorene Kettler, St. John Lutheran Church, Cypress, Texas

CURRIED FILET OF CHICKEN WITH BROCCOLI

4 filets chicken breasts or legs
1/4 t. Accent
1/4 t. pepper
Corn oil
1—1 lb. pkg. frozen broccoli
1 can cream of chicken soup

1/2 cup mayonnaise
1 t. lemon juice
1/4 t. curry powder
1 cup cheddar cheese, shredded
Paprika

Sprinkle Accent and pepper over chicken. Saute' chicken in oil for 6 minutes. Drain on paper towels. Place chicken in 2-quart casserole. Cook broccoli 4–5 minutes. Arrange broccoli around chicken. Mix soup, mayonnaise, lemon juice, and curry powder. Pour over chicken, leaving an edge of broccoli for color. Sprinkle with cheese and paprika. Bake uncovered at 375°F. for 30 minutes. Serves 4.

Judy Stepulitis, Christ's United Lutheran Church, Gordon, Pennsylvania

CURRY GLAZED CHICKEN WITH BAKED RICE

2 T. butter or margarine
1/4 cup honey
3 T. prepared mustard

1 t. curry
1/2 t. salt
1 chicken (fryer), cut up

Set oven at 375 °F. Put butter in bottom of 13''x9''x2'' pan; place in oven to melt. When melted, remove from oven. Stir in honey, mustard, curry, and salt. Add cut up chicken and coat well. Bake uncovered 45 minutes. Baste once or twice during baking.

BAKED RICE

1 cup regular rice
1 t. salt

1 T. butter or margarine
2-1/2 cups boiling water

Combine rice with salt and butter. Put in 4–6 cup baking dish. Stir in the boiling water. Cover and bake 45–50 minutes.

Both items can be baked at the same time as they require about the same time for completion.

Margaret Butler, Euclid Lutheran Church, Euclid, Ohio

CHICKEN CURRY

3 T. butter
1/4 cup onion, minced
1 t. or more curry powder
3 T. flour
3/4 t. salt
3/4 t. sugar

1/8 t. ground ginger
1 cup chicken broth
1 cup milk
2 cups cooked chicken pieces
1/2 t. lemon juice

Melt butter over low heat in heavy saucepan. Saute´ onion and curry powder in butter. Blend in flour and seasonings. Cook over medium heat until mixture is smooth and bubbly. Stir in chicken broth and milk. Bring to boil for 1 minute. Add chicken and lemon juice; heat through. Serve over rice. Yield: 6–7 servings.

If condiments are desired, use chopped peanuts, raisins, coconut, chopped boiled egg.

Rev. Beth Ann Miller, First Presbyterian Church, Morganton, North Carolina

CHICKEN-CHESTNUT SOUFFLE'

9 slices white bread, crust removed
4 cups cooked chicken, cubed
1 small onion, chopped
1—8 oz. can sliced mushrooms, drained
1—8 oz. can sliced water chestnuts, drained
9 slices process sharp cheddar cheese

1/2 cup mayonnaise
4 eggs, well beaten
2 cups milk
1 t. salt
1 can cream of mushroom soup
1 can cream of celery soup
1—2 oz. jar chopped pimiento, drained
2 cups buttered coarse bread crumbs

Line a buttered 13''x9''x2'' baking dish with bread; top with chicken, onion, mushrooms, water chestnuts, and cheese. Combine mayonnaise, eggs, milk, and salt, beating well; pour over cheese. Combine soup and pimiento, stirring well; spoon over casserole. Cover and place in refrigerator overnight. Bake, uncovered, at 350°F. for 40 minutes. Remove from oven, top with bread crumbs. Return to oven and bake an additional 15–20 minutes or until set.

Bonnie Tabor, Grace United Methodist Church, Gallipolis, Ohio

CHICKEN PILAF

1-1/2 cups Minute Rice, uncooked
1—10-1/2 oz. can condensed cream of mushroom soup
1-1/4 cups boiling water
1/4 cup dry sherry

1/2 envelope dry onion soup mix
2 T. chopped canned pimiento
5 small chicken breasts
Butter or margarine, melted
Salt and pepper
Paprika

In a 2-quart rectangular casserole, combine first 6 ingredients. Put chicken on top of rice mixture. Brush with butter. Season with salt, pepper, and paprika. Cover. Bake in oven at 375°F. for 1-1/4 hours. Makes 5 servings.

Sister Anne Mary Lochner, OSU, St. Mary Church, Louisville, Kentucky

CHICKEN CONTINENTAL

3 lbs. chicken
1/4 cup butter
1-2/3 cups rice, uncooked
1 T. parsley
1/4 cup celery, cut

1 can cream of mushroom soup
1 t. salt
Dash of pepper
1-2/3 cups water

Cut chicken into serving pieces and fry slowly in butter until nicely browned. Place in baking dish with rice, parsley, and celery. Put soup, salt, pepper, and water in frying pan and bring to boil. Pour over other ingredients and bake 1-1/2–2 hours at 350°F.

Mabel Warfel, Orrville Christian and Missionary Alliance Church, Orrville, Ohio

CHICKEN ALMOND CASSEROLE

2/3 cup Pepperidge Farm
 stuffing
1 pkg. frozen French green
 beans, partly cooked
2–3 T. slivered blanched
 almonds

Sliced chicken breasts, cooked
1-1/2 cup canned gravy or
 1 can cream of mushroom
 soup with 1/2 cup water
1-1/2 cups stuffing crumbs
2 T. butter, melted

In greased shallow casserole arrange in layers: Stuffing, green beans (partly cooked), almonds; then sliced or diced chicken or turkey. Pour gravy or soup over all. Now moisten 1-1/2 cups stuffing crumbs with 1/4 cup hot water and 2 tablespoons melted butter. Spread over casserole. Bake at 400°F. for 30 minutes.

Catherine Jenkins, St. Mary Church, Louisville, Kentucky

CHICKEN CASSEROLE

This recipe and its variations is really used a lot around Grace United Methodist Church because it's so easy to serve with salads, rolls and butter, and a simple dessert.

2 cups cooked chicken, cubed
1 pt. milk or like amount broth
1—7 oz. pkg. macaroni,
 uncooked

1 can cream of celery soup
3 hard cooked eggs, diced
1/2 lb. Velveeta cheese

Mix all together and put in refrigerator overnight. Take out 1 hour before baking. Cover top with crushed corn flakes, if desired. Bake 1 hour at 375°F.

NOTE: Ham may be substituted for chicken; however, do use milk instead of ham broth, because of salt content of ham broth. You may also substitute cream of chicken or cream of mushroom soup, if desired.

Betty Kincaid, Grace United Methodist Church, Geneseo, Illinois

BUSY DAY CHICKEN AND DRESSING CASSEROLE

2-1/2 cups chicken, diced
1—8 oz. pkg. Pepperidge Farm
  Herb Seasoned Stuffing
1/2 cup celery, chopped
1 stick butter, melted
1 cup water
1/2 cup onions, chopped

1/2 cup mayonnaise
3/4 t. salt
2 eggs
1-1/2 cup milk
1 can condensed cream of
  mushroom soup
Grated cheese for top

Mix stuffing with butter and water. Toss lightly to blend. Place half of mixture in buttered dish. Mix chicken, onion, celery, mayonnaise, and salt. Spread over mixture; top with remaining bread crumb mixture. Beat eggs slightly and add milk. Pour over mixture. Cover with foil and leave in refrigerator overnight. Take out 1 hour before baking; spread soup over top. Bake uncovered at 325°F. for 40 minutes. Remove from oven, sprinkle with cheese and cook for 10 minutes. Serves 8–10 people (or more if cut in smaller squares).

Mrs. J.H. Sweeney, First Baptist Church, Nashville, Tennessee

CHICKEN AND DRESSING CASSEROLE

3–4 cups cooked chicken, diced
1 cup dry bread crumbs
2 T. butter; 1/2 cup butter;
  1 cup butter
3/4 cup celery, diced
1/2 cup onion, finely chopped
2 T. parsley, chopped
6 cups day old bread, cubed

Salt and pepper to taste
1 t. poultry seasoning
Approximately 4-1/2 cups
  chicken broth
1 cup flour
1 cup milk
4 eggs

Saute' bread crumbs in 2 tablespoons butter to brown lightly; set aside. Saute' celery, onion, and parsley in 1/2 cup butter for 5 minutes. Toss in bread cubes. Add salt and pepper to taste and poultry seasoning. Sprinkle with 3 tablespoons of the chicken broth; set aside.

Melt 1 cup butter in large pan; whisk in flour. Gradually add 4 cups broth and 1 cup milk, whisking constantly. Add 2 teaspoons salt; cook until thickened. Whisk eggs well in small bowl. Add a little of the sauce to eggs; whisk well; add back to sauce in pan. Cook 3–4 minutes, stirring well. Turn bread cube mixture into a greased 2-1/2– quart casserole. Cover with half of the sauce, then cover with the diced chicken. Cover with sauce. Sprinkle crumbs evenly over top. Bake at 350°F. for 20–25 minutes.

April Lemons, Rinconada Hills Christian Church, Los Gatos, California

SEAFOOD

FLOUNDER BAKE

Flounder
Sliced tomatoes
Juice of 1/2 lemon
Salt, pepper, and oregano to taste

Swiss cheese, shredded
Cheddar cheese, shredded
Parmesan cheese

Slice tomatoes and line bottom of pan. Wash flounder and pat dry; lay on tomatoes. Salt, pepper, and oregano to taste, and squeeze juice of half a lemon. Put a layer of shredded Swiss cheese and cheddar cheese on top. Sprinkle a little Parmesan cheese on top. Bake at 350°F. for 35 minutes. No need to turn.

Helen Walker, Middlebrook Pike United Methodist Church, Knoxville, Tennessee

FLOUNDER CASSEROLE

1-1/2 lbs. filet of flounder
1/4 cup dry white wine or
white grape juice
8–10 slices white mild cheese
(colby or Monterey Jack)

1/2 T. lemon juice
3/4 cup Italian seasoned bread
crumbs
1/4 cup Parmesan cheese, grated
1/2 stick butter or margarine

Place flounder in glass casserole dish or pie plate. Dot with pats of butter or margarine. Add wine or grape juice and cover fish with slices of mild cheese. Add lemon juice. Melt 1/2 stick of butter in fry pan over low heat. After melted, stir in bread crumbs and Parmesan cheese. Stir until well buttered. Sprinkle over entire casserole. Bake at 350°F. for 1/2 hour until crumbs are golden brown. Serves 2–3.

Elizabeth M. Loeffler, Roxborough Presbyterian Church, Philadelphia, Pennsylvania

E-Z STUFFED TURBOT

Turbot filets (2 filets serves 2)
1 can cream of mushroom soup
1 can (or fresh) crab meat or shrimp

Fresh mushrooms, sliced
(about 4 large for 2 servings)

In buttered casserole layer half of filets. Add crab meat, then cover with 1/2 can of undiluted cream of mushroom soup and half of sliced mushrooms. Place remaining turbot filets on top and add balance of mushroom soup and mushrooms. Bake uncovered at 325°F. for 1-1/4 hours.

Gene Gador, First Congregational United Church of Christ, Oroville, California

CURRIED FISH AND CHIP BAKE

1—14 oz. pkg. frozen breaded
  fish filets or frozen batter
  dipped fish
1—16 oz. pkg. frozen fried
  crinkle cut potatoes
1—10-3/4 oz. can cream of celery soup

3/4 cup milk
1/3 cup mayonnaise or
  salad dressing
1 t. curry powder

Arrange fish filets on bottom of greased 13''x9''x2'' baking dish. Arrange French fries on fish. Combine soup, milk, mayonnaise, and curry powder. Pour mixture over fish and French fries. Bake uncovered for about 45 minutes or until bubbly. Garnish with parsley sprig.

Margaret Butler, Euclid Lutheran Church, Euclid, Ohio

SCALLOP CASSEROLE

2 lbs. scallops
2 cups dry white wine (Chablis)
1/4 t. salt
1/2 t. Accent
1/4 t. Accent
1/2 lb. fresh mushrooms

1 T. parsley, chopped
1 T. water
2 T. lemon juice
1/4 cup heavy cream
2 egg yolks

Do the following with the first 4 ingredients: Bring to a boil and simmer 10 minutes, drain scallops and reserve liquid (set aside).

Meanwhile, saute' the next 5 ingredients in 3 tablespoons butter. Cook 8–10 minutes and pour this mixture over scallops.

Heat 1/4 cup butter and add 1/4 cup flour; heat until bubbling and remove from heat. Gradually add reserved liquid from scallops and bring to a boil, stirring constantly. Boil for 2 minutes. Remove from heat and stir in 1/4 cup heavy cream and 2 well beaten egg yolks. Mix well. Pour sauce over scallops and put into casserole dish. Sprinkle bread crumbs on top. Bake at 450°F. for 8–10 minutes.

Kathleen Shaker, St. Jerome Church, New Britain, Connecticut

JENNIFER'S CRAB SPINACH CASSEROLE

1 lb. crab meat
2 pkgs. chopped frozen spinach
8 oz. Monterey Jack cheese,
   shredded
1/2 cup herbed bread crumbs
1 T. Old Bay seasoning
3 T. sour cream
1 T. Worcestershire sauce

1 T. parsley, chopped
1 T. baking powder
2 eggs, beaten
1 pkg. Wise green onion
   dip mix
1 pkg. Good Seasons Italian
   salad dressing mix
1/2 carton Egg Beaters

Soak bread crumbs in milk for 10 minutes. Mix rest of ingredients, except cheese. Place in large casserole dish. Top with cheese and pour Egg Beaters over ingredients. Cook in a 375°F. oven for 30–45 minutes or until eggs are set. Or cook in microwave oven at 80% power for 8–10 minutes or until eggs are set.

This casserole is excellent and tastes like crab; the spinach takes on the crab flavor.

Jennifer Mahan, Yeocomico Episcopal Church, Tucker Hill, Virginia

ISLAND CRAB CASSEROLE

1 lb. or 2—6 oz. cans crab meat
8–10 hard boiled eggs, chopped
1 cup bread crumbs
1/2 cup evaporated milk
1/2 cup cooked celery,
   finely chopped
Small amount minced onion
   (optional)

Salt and pepper to taste
1 cup salad dressing
   (or 1 cup mayonnaise with
   1 t. vinegar)
TOPPING
1 stick margarine
Approximately 4 oz. Ritz
   crackers

Either soak bread crumbs in the milk or toss gently in a blender. Cook celery and onion in a small amount of water (just enough to cover; boil about 10 minutes). Drain, if necessary. Mix all ingredients together and put in buttered casserole dish.

Melt margarine in saucepan and add enough crumbled Ritz crackers to soak up margarine. Spread over casserole and bake at 350°F. for approximately 30 minutes or until lightly browned and thoroughly heated. Serves 6–8 and may be frozen.

Carol Marvel, St. James' Episcopal Church, Charleston, South Carolina

CRAB MEAT COBBLER

1/2 cup shortening
1/2 cup green pepper
1/2 cup onion
1/2 cup flour
1 t. dry mustard
1/2 t. Accent

1 cup milk
1 cup cheddar cheese, shredded
1 can crab meat
1-1/2 cups drained tomatoes
2 t. Worcestershire sauce
1/2 t. salt

Melt 1/2 cup shortening. Add green pepper and onion, cook until tender. Blend in flour, mustard, Accent, milk, and cheddar cheese. Cook, stir, until cheese melts. Add remaining ingredients. Blend and pour into 2-quart casserole.

BISCUIT TOPPING

1 cup flour
2 t. baking powder
1/2 t. salt

1/4 cup cheese, shredded
2 T. shortening
1/2 cup milk

Sift flour, baking powder, and salt together. Add cheese. Cut in shortening until mixture resembles cornmeal. Add milk, mix until flour is dampened. Drop by rounded teaspoons on top of crab meat mixture. Bake at 450°F. for 15–20 minutes.

Virginia Chatto, Pratt Memorial United Methodist Church, Rockland, Maine

SHRIMP CRAB CASSEROLE

1—6 oz. can shrimp
1—6 oz. can crab meat
1/2 cup butter
1/4 cup flour
1/4 cup cheese, grated

1 cup milk
2 T. sherry
2 cups soft bread crumbs
Salt, pepper, and paprika

Cook seafoods in 1/4 cup butter 4–5 minutes, stirring constantly. Add salt and pepper to taste. Blend in flour and gradually add milk, stirring until thickened. Add sherry, and more salt and pepper, if needed. Pour into a shallow 1-quart baking dish. Melt remaining 1/4 cup butter; mix with bread crumbs and grated cheese. Sprinkle over top of cream mixture. Sprinkle with paprika. Bake at 350°F. for 15 minutes or until light brown.

Sandy Edie, Sunnyside United Methodist Church, Kalamazoo, Michigan

CREOLE SHRIMP

1 lb. shrimp, raw and cleaned
1 large onion, chopped
1 large green pepper, chopped
1/2 cup ketchup

1 cup water
1 large T. flour
1 large T. bacon grease

Saute' onion and pepper in bacon grease. When light tan in color, add shrimp and stir until pink. Add flour, then ketchup and water. Stir; serve over rice.

Frances Basnight, Broad Street Christian Church, New Bern, North Carolina

SHRIMP JAMBALAYA

1 lb. fresh or frozen shrimp,
   cleaned
1 cup green pepper, chopped
1/2 cup onion, chopped
2 cloves garlic, finely chopped
1/4 cup melted fat or oil
1 qt. or 2 cans tomatoes
1-1/2 cups water

1 cup rice, uncooked
1/2 t. whole thyme, crushed
1 t. salt
Dash pepper
1 bay leaf
1/4 cup parsley, chopped
   or dried flakes

Thaw frozen shrimp. Cook until tender pepper, onion, and garlic in fat at 300°F. Add remaining ingredients except parsley and shrimp. Reduce to 200°F., cover and cook 15–20 minutes, stirring occasionally. Add parsley and shrimp. Cook for 15 minutes longer, still covered. Remove bay leaf. Serves 6.

For Chicken Jambalaya, substitute chicken for shrimp.

Glenda Gouge, Bethany Baptist Church, Snellville, Georgia

FIVE CAN MOCK CHOW MEIN

1 can chow mein vegetables
1 can chow mein noodles,
   save part for top
1 can tuna, chunk style

1 can cream of mushroom soup
1 can cream of chicken soup or
   celery soup

Mix together in casserole dish; sprinkle dry noodles on top. Bake at 350°F. for 45–60 minutes.

To fancy up, add a few cashews or slivered almonds on top. For more servings, use family size tuna and two cans of everything.

Agnes Tilly, Kent Lutheran Church, Kent, Washington

MEATLESS DISHES

SARAH SASSER'S SPINACH LASAGNE SQUARES

Used to serve 300 people for Concord Presbytery Meeting at First Presbyterian Church in Morganton, North Carolina

1 medium onion, chopped
1/2 green pepper
2 garlic cloves, minced
2 T. vegetable oil
1—28 oz. can tomatoes
1—6 oz. can tomato paste
1/4 cup parsley
1/2 t. oregano
1 bay leaf
1—8 oz. pkg. lasagne noodles

1—10 oz. pkg. frozen chopped
    spinach, drained
1 egg
1 lb. ricotta or low fat
    cottage cheese
3/4 cup Parmesan cheese, grated
1 t. salt
1/4 t. pepper
8 oz. mozzarella cheese, grated

Saute' onion, green pepper, and garlic in oil until golden brown; stir often. Add tomatoes (chopped or mashed), tomato paste, parsley, oregano, and bay leaf. Simmer uncovered 20 minutes. Cook noodles according to package directions; drain. Combine spinach, ricotta or cottage cheese, egg, 1/4 cup Parmesan cheese, salt, and pepper.

Spoon a third of the tomato sauce in bottom of lasagne dish or 9''x13'' pan. Cover with a third of the lasagne noodles, half the spinach-ricotta filling, half the mozzarella, and 1/4 cup Parmesan. Repeat layers, using half remaining sauce and noodles and all remaining fillings. Top with remaining noodles, sauce, Parmesan, and mozzarella. Bake at 350°F. for 45 minutes. Let stand for a few minutes before cutting into squares for serving. Serves 6 and freezes well.

Mrs. Pam Daniel, First Presbyterian Church, Morganton, North Carolina

KUGEL

8 oz. noodles (any kind)
8 oz. cream cheese
1 stick margarine
4 eggs

1 cup sugar
1 can evaporated milk
1/2 cup fresh milk
1 t. vanilla

Cook noodles according to directions, drain and pour into 9''x13'' buttered pan. Cream cheese, margarine, eggs, sugar, milk, and vanilla. Pour over noodles, sprinkle with cinnamon and bake at 325°F. for 1 hour.

Mrs. June Phillips, First Baptist Church, Clarion, Pennsylvania

PECAN MEATBALLS

1 cup pecans, finely ground
2 cups coarse bread crumbs
1-1/2 cups longhorn cheese,
   grated
1 large onion, chopped
4 eggs

2–3 t. Worcestershire sauce
1/2 t. sage
1 t. paprika
Juice from 1 clove garlic,
   pressed
Pinch of salt, if desired

Mix all together, roll into small balls and roll in flour. Pan fry until brown and put into pot. Cover with sauce and simmer 30–45 minutes. Serve with cooked spaghetti. Yield: 6–8 servings.

SAUCE

1/2 small can tomato paste
2 large cans tomato sauce

1 t. sugar
1/4 t. garlic powder

Mix all ingredients together.

Irene Cortez, Wichita Seventh Day Adventist South Church, Wichita, Kansas

STUFFED MUSHROOMS

A high-protein vegetarian main dish

12 large fresh mushrooms
1 small onion
1/2 cup canned garbanzos,
   drained
1 stick margarine
3/4 cup fine bread crumbs
   (whole wheat is better)
2 T. wheat germ

1/2 t. garlic powder
2 t. dried parsley
Salt and pepper to taste
1 t. Dijon style mustard
1/2 cup mozzarella cheese,
   grated
Parmesan cheese, grated

Wash and dry mushrooms. Remove and trim stems and arrange caps on a lightly oiled sheet. Chop onion slightly in food processor. Add garbanzos and mushroom stems; chop all very fine. Melt margarine in medium skillet, add vegetables and saute' slightly. Stir in bread crumbs, wheat germ, and seasonings. Remove from heat and stir in mustard and mozzarella cheese. Using spoon and fingers, mound stuffing into caps. Sprinkle with Parmesan cheese. Bake at 325 °F. for 25–30 minutes.

Strict ''vegans'' may omit cheeses; they're still good.

Carolyn Mitchell, First Baptist Church, Macon, Georgia

MICH'S MACARONI AND CHEESE

1 cup small elbow macaroni   1 cup milk
1 t. salt   1 egg
1 T. oil
10 oz. sharp cheese (or your choice)

Put macaroni and salt in pot and add about twice as much water as macaroni. Add oil. Bring to a boil, stirring occasionally. When boiling well, put lid on and set off heat. Leave for about 10 minutes. Grate cheese in 9'' square casserole. Lay aside about a third of the cheese. Stir macaroni and pour it and any liquid in it into the casserole with cheese. Mix together. In pot where macaroni cooked, beat egg and add milk. Stir until mixed and pour over macaroni and cheese. If milk mixture doesn't almost cover macaroni and cheese, add more milk. Add remaining cheese on top. Dot with margarine. Bake at about 400°F. until lightly browned. Serves about 6.

Mich Riddle, First Baptist Church, Taylors, South Carolina

PASTA SHELLS WITH PEPPERS

1 lb. small pasta shells   1 onion, thinly sliced
3 green and/or red peppers,   4 small tomatoes,
  halved, seeded, deribbed,   peeled, seeded, and diced
  and cut into strips   1 large bunch basil
Oil   Salt and pepper
Butter   Parmesan cheese

Cover the bottom of a frying pan with oil and a little butter. Saute' onion slices until they turn pale gold. Add peppers; cook over fairly high heat, stirring frequently. When peppers begin to become tender, add tomatoes, basil, salt, and pepper. Reduce the heat; cover pan and cook 15 minutes. Remove lid and let the water from the tomatoes evaporate.

While peppers and tomatoes are simmering, cook pasta shells aldente and drain them well. Combine peppers and tomato mixture with cooked shells and add Parmesan cheese generously. Serves 4–5 people.

Deborah L. Plimmer, Eastern Heights Church, Cleburne, Texas

GLORIOUS MACARONI

1—8 oz. pkg. seashell macaroni
1 T. butter or margarine
1/4 cup onion, chopped
1—2 oz. jar diced pimiento,
    drained
2 cups (8 oz.) cheddar cheese,
    shredded

1—10-3/4 oz. can cream of
    mushroom soup, undiluted
1/2 cup mayonnaise
1—2-1/2 oz. jar sliced
    mushrooms
1/2 green pepper

Cook macaroni in a Dutch oven according to package directions; drain. Melt butter in a small skillet. Add onion and pimiento, and saute' until onion is crisp and tender. Combine macaroni, onion mixture, and remaining ingredients; mix well. Spoon into a lightly greased 2-quart shallow casserole. Bake at 350°F. for 30 minutes. Top with 3/4 stick butter and 1 cup crushed Ritz crackers or Cheez-its. Yield: 6 servings.

Sherry Hancock, Palestine Baptist Church, Campbellsville, Kentucky

SPANISH RICE

1 large can whole cooked
    tomatoes
1-1/2–2 cups rice, cooked
3/4 lb. cheddar cheese,
    cut into small pieces

6 pieces bacon, cooked
1/4 cup green pepper, chopped
1/4 cup onion, chopped
Salt and pepper to taste

Warm tomatoes in saucepan. Add rice, cheese (reserve few slices for top), bacon, green pepper, onion, salt, and pepper. Mix well. Fill casserole dish, top with slices of cheese, cracker crumbs and dot with butter. Bake 375°F. for 20 minutes until bubbly. May be multiplied.

Mrs. Richard I. Gourley, First Congregational Church, Hopkinton, New Hampshire

Vegetables
and
Side Dishes

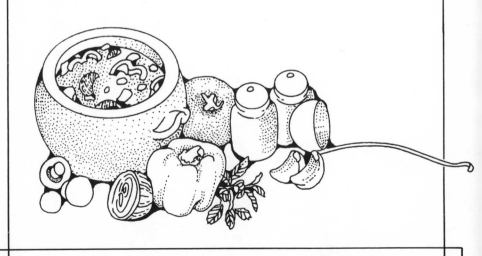

VEGETABLES AND SIDE DISHES

BUTTERSCOTCH CARROTS

2 cups carrots, pared and cut
   into pieces
4 T. butter
2 t. all-purpose flour
1/4 cup orange juice

1/3 cup brown sugar,
   firmly packed
1/4 t. salt
Generous pinch of cinnamon
1/4 t. vanilla

Steam carrots; drain. In a small saucepan over low heat melt butter. Stir in flour. Add remaining ingredients except vanilla. Stir constantly until smooth and slightly thickened. Stir in vanilla and carrots. Reheat if necessary. Makes 2 large servings.

Mary Stovall, First Presbyterian Church, Port Angeles, Washington

ZESTY CARROTS

8 cooked carrots, cut into
   8 sticks each
1/4 cup liquid from cooked
   carrots
2 T. horseradish
2 T. onion, grated
1/2 cup mayonnaise

1/2 t. salt
1/4 t. white pepper
Bread crumbs
Paprika
Parsley
Butter

Cook carrots until barely tender. Mix together next 6 ingredients and pour over carrots. Sprinkle with bread crumbs, paprika, and parsley and dot with butter on top. Bake at 350°F. for 20–25 minutes.

Joan Winter, St. Mark United Methodist Church, Atlanta, Georgia

CORN CUSTARD

2 cups milk
2 cups whole corn
2 T. butter, melted
3 eggs, well beaten

1 T. sugar
1 t. salt
1/4 t. pepper

Add milk, corn, butter, sugar, and seasonings to beaten eggs. Turn into buttered casserole and bake at 350°F. for 45 minutes or until custard is set. Serves 6.

Ruth E. Rowe, West Side United Methodist Church, Wichita, Kansas

PENNSYLVANIA DUTCH STYLE GREEN BEANS

3 strips bacon
1 small onion, sliced
2 t. cornstarch
1/4 t. salt
1/4 t. dry mustard

1—1 lb. can cut green beans
1 T. brown sugar
1 T. vinegar
1 hard cooked egg, sliced

Fry bacon in skillet until crisp. Remove bacon and crumble. Drain off all but 1 tablespoon drippings. Add onion and brown lightly. Stir in cornstarch, salt, and dry mustard. Drain beans, reserving 1/2 cup liquid. Stir reserved liquid into skillet. Cook, stirring until mixture boils. Blend in brown sugar and vinegar. Add green beans and heat thoroughly. Turn into serving dish and garnish with egg and crumbled bacon. Makes about 4 servings.

Eleanore L. Bates, Hope Reformed Church, South Haven, Michigan

BEST EVER BAKED BEANS

9 strips bacon, fried
1/4 cup onion, chopped
Bacon drippings
2—16 oz. cans pork and beans
1/2 cup ketchup

1/4 cup maple syrup
1 t. dry mustard
1/2 t. chili powder
Dash of Tabasco sauce
1/2 t. Worcestershire sauce

Fry bacon. From drippings, saute' onion. Combine all ingredients except 4 slices of bacon to be placed on top. Crumble the other bacon into the beans. Bake 350°F. for 45 minutes.

Shirley Kirkland, Davis Chapel Baptist Church, Austell, Georgia

GRAM'S BEANS

1 medium onion
1 t. salt
8 T. sweetening (brown sugar, syrup, molasses, divided evenly)
1/4 lb. salt pork

1 t. dry mustard
2 cups dry beans (use as many different kinds of beans as possible such as Jacob's cattle, soldier's beans, kidney, pea, etc.)

Soak beans overnight and simmer for 1/2 hour in the morning. Drain and rinse well. Put pork and onion in bottom of pot and add beans. Mix remaining ingredients with hot water and pour over beans, adding enough water so that you can see it. Cover and cook at 325°F. for 6 hours, adding hot water twice during cooking. Add *no* water in last hour.

Lois Flewelling, Trinity Baptist Church, Lynnfield, Massachusetts

EVERYBODY'S FAVORITE CABBAGE NOODLES

Favorite for church picnics, dinners, and showers

1 lb. medium egg noodles
2 sticks margarine
1/2 cup caraway seeds
1 small head cabbage, shredded

2 onions, chopped
1/4 cup water
Salt and pepper to taste

While noodles are cooking, according to directions, melt margarine in large kettle. Sauté onions until clear. Add chopped cabbage, caraway seeds, and water. Cover and cook until cabbage is done, but not over-cooked. Drain noodles and add to cabbage mixture and serve. Delicious.

Jeannette Roy, Bethesda Full Gospel Tabernacle, Tonawanda, New York

EVERYBODY-LOVES-IT CABBAGE CASSEROLE

1/2 cup margarine
1-1/2 cups cracker crumbs
4 T. butter
3 T. flour

1-1/2 cups milk
5 oz. jar Old English cheese
3 cups cooked cabbage,
    barely tender

Melt margarine, add cracker crumbs and press in bottom of 9"x12" pan, saving some for topping. Place drained cabbage over crumb bottom. Melt butter in a saucepan; add flour, milk, and cheese. Bring to a simmer and stir until cheese is melted. Pour over cabbage and top with remaining crumbs. Bake at 350°F. for 35 minutes.

Dorothy Hall, Salem United Church of Christ, Louisville, Kentucky

SWEET 'N' SOUR GREEN BEANS

2 cans green beans
3 slices bacon
Onion to taste
1/3 cup water

1/3 cup vinegar
1/3 cup sugar
1 T. cornstarch

Cut bacon into chunks and sauté with onion until brown. Drain off grease. Add water, vinegar, and sugar; stir. Make paste with cornstarch and add to mixture. Cook over medium heat and allow to boil until thick. Pour over heated and drained green beans.

Rosa Acheson, First Church of the Nazarene, Independence, Kansas

SHOE PEG CORN CASSEROLE

1—12 oz. can shoe peg corn, drained
1/2 cup onion, chopped
1—10-3/4 oz. can cream of celery soup

1—15 oz. can French cut green beans, drained
1/2 cup cheddar cheese, grated
1/2 cup sour cream

Combine corn, beans, soup, onion, cheese and sour cream. Place in a greased casserole dish. Spread topping over vegetable mixture. Bake at 350°F. for 35 minutes. Serves 8, is easily doubled and will fill a 9"x13" container.

TOPPING

1 roll (35) Ritz or Hi-Ho crackers, crushed

1/2 cup slivered almonds
1/2 cup margarine, melted

Mix ingredients together.

Alice L. Brownell, Wentzville United Methodist Church, Wentzville, Missouri

POTLUCK VEGETABLE CASSEROLE

1—17 oz. can whole kernel corn
1—10 oz. pkg. frozen cauliflower, cooked
1—10 oz. pkg. frozen cut broccoli, cooked
1—4 oz. can sliced mushrooms
1—17 oz. can cream style corn

2 cups Swiss cheese, shredded
1—10-3/4 oz. can condensed cream of celery soup
2 T. butter or margarine
1-1/2 cups soft rye or white bread crumbs

Drain whole kernel corn, cooked cauliflower, cooked broccoli, and mushrooms. Cut up large pieces of cauliflower. Combine cream style corn, cheese, and soup. Fold in drained vegetables. Turn into a 12"x7-1/2"x2" baking dish. Melt butter; toss with crumbs. Sprinkle atop mixture. Bake uncovered in a 375°F. oven for 30–35 minutes or until hot.

Violet Jefferson, Poplar Springs Church of God, Richmond, Virginia

BROCCOLI SPEARS WITH CHEESY RICE BALLS

3 cups rice, cooked and cooled
3 eggs, slightly beaten
1/3 cup all-purpose flour
1/2 t. salt

1/4 t. pepper
3 oz. American cheese, cubed
1/2 cup cracker crumbs,
  finely crushed

Combine first 5 ingredients. Cut American cheese into 1/2" cubes. Form rice into balls with wet hands and shape mixture around a cheese cube. Roll rice balls in cracker crumbs. Fry rice balls in a 7" skillet with 1/2" of cooking oil at 365°F. Fry 4–5 at a time, turning once and draining on a paper towel. Keep warm.

SAUCE

2 T. onion, chopped
2 T. butter
2 T. all-purpose flour

1/2 t. salt
Dash of pepper
1-1/4 cups milk

In small saucepan cook onion in butter until tender but not brown. Add flour, salt, and pepper. Add milk all at once. Cook and stir until thickened. Cook 1 minute more. Add any remaining cheese cubes, stirring until melted.

To serve, arrange rice balls in center of platter, placing cooked broccoli spears around platter. Pour sauce over rice balls. Serves 4.

Diane Copley, Fairview Baptist Church, Statesville, North Carolina

BROCCOLI-RICE CASSEROLE

4-1/2 cups rice, precooked
2—10 oz. pkgs. frozen chopped
  broccoli
1 cup celery, chopped
1/2 cup onion, chopped

2 cans condensed cream of
  mushroom soup
1 cup milk
1—16 oz. jar American cheese
  spread

Cook rice and broccoli according to package directions; drain well and set aside. Cook celery and onion in margarine until tender, then combine soup, milk, and cheese. Stir in rice, broccoli, and celery mixture and pour into two 2-quart casseroles. Bake in 350°F. oven for 45 minutes. Serves 12 and can be made ahead and refrigerated until ready to use.

Mrs. Rosalee Tanner, Six Mile Creek Baptist Church, Tampa, Florida

BROCCOLI CASSEROLE

2—10 oz. pkgs. frozen broccoli,
  steamed or microwaved
1 cup mayonnaise
1 can cream of mushroom soup

2 eggs
2 cups cheddar cheese,
  grated
1 cup cheese crackers, crumbled

Place cooked broccoli in 2-quart casserole dish. Mix together mayonnaise, soup, eggs, and 1 cup cheese. Pour over broccoli and mix together. Sprinkle crackers and remaining cheese over top. Bake uncovered in a 350°F. oven for 1 hour.

Jane Wilson, First Christian Church, San Bernardino, California

SWEET 'N' SOUR BRUSSEL SPROUTS

3 cups fresh or 2—9 oz. pkgs.
  frozen brussel sprouts
8 slices bacon
2 T. vinegar

2 t. sugar
1/2 t. salt
1/4 t. garlic powder
1/8 t. pepper

Wash fresh brussel sprouts; cut off any wilted leaves. Cook covered in small amount of boiling salted water for 10–15 minutes or until tender (Or cook frozen brussel sprouts according to package directions). Drain. Meanwhile, in a skillet fry bacon until crisp; drain, reserving 1/4 cup drippings. Crumble bacon and set aside. To reserved drippings add vinegar, sugar, salt, garlic powder, and pepper. Add brussel sprouts; stir until heated through and well coated. Sprinkle with the crumbled bacon. Makes 6–8 servings.

Sue Bobbitt, Abney Street Church of God, St. Albans, West Virginia

CRUSTY CAULIFLOWER AU GRATIN

1 large head cauliflower
1/2 lb. cheddar cheese, shredded
5 cups medium white sauce (Tabasco optional)

4 slices bread, cubed, dry
5 T. butter

Cook cauliflower and separate. Put in a greased 9"x13" pan. Stir cheese into white sauce and pour over cauliflower. Add cubed bread to melted butter. Put on top of cauliflower. Sprinkle with paprika. Bake at 350°F. for 30 minutes.

Marie Hamm, Calvary Baptist Church, Fargo, North Dakota

EGGPLANT SCALLOP

4 cups (1 medium) eggplant,
  diced, peeled
1/4 cup butter or margarine
2 eggs, beaten
1 cup milk
1/2 t. salt

2—3 oz. pkgs. cream cheese,
  softened
1-1/2 cups soft bread crumbs
  (2 slices bread)
2 T. butter or margarine, melted
1/4 t. onion powder

In medium skillet cook eggplant in the 1/4 cup butter or margarine for 8–10 minutes. Set aside. In a bowl combine beaten eggs, milk, and salt; blend into cream cheese. Stir in eggplant. Turn into 10''x6''x2'' baking dish. Combine bread crumbs, remaining 2 tablespoons butter or margarine, and onion powder. Sprinkle crumb mixture over casserole. Bake in 350°F. oven for 25–30 minutes. Test custard-fashion by inserting knife until it comes out clean. Let stand 5 minutes. Serve and enjoy!

Mrs. Remo (Dot) Pedicini, The Congregational Church of Topsfield, Topsfield, Massachusetts

BAKED SQUASH

3 strips bacon
6 medium yellow squash
1/2 onion, chopped

3 oz. cheddar cheese, shredded
Toasted bread crumbs

Fry 3 strips bacon; crumble. Chop squash into medium chunks. Cover squash and onions with water and bring to boil. Cook until half done. Place in baking dish. Add cheese, salt and pepper to taste. Top with crumbs and bacon. Bake at 350°F. for 30 minutes.

Martina (Marty) Wohkittel, Covenant Presbyterian Church, Carrollton, Texas

CREAMY SQUASH CASSEROLE

1-1/2 lbs. yellow squash or
  zucchini, sliced and steamed
  5 minutes
1 can cream of chicken soup
1/2 cup mayonnaise

1 cup sour cream
1—2 oz. jar pimientos, diced
2 medium onions, diced small
1/2 box stuffing croutons
1/4 lb. margarine, melted

Melt margarine and pour over croutons. Put two-thirds of the croutons in a 2-quart casserole; add the squash. Mix all other ingredients and pour over squash. Top with rest of croutons. Cover and bake at 350°F. for 30 minutes or until bubbly.

Mrs. Selma M. Sheasley, St. John's Episcopal Church, Sharon, Pennsylvania

ZUCCHINI, TOMATOES, AND BACON

10 slices bacon, cut in
   1/2'' pieces
1-1/2 lbs. zucchini (or two),
   cubed

1 qt. tomatoes
1 t. salt
1 t. dried basil leaves
1 onion, chopped

Fry bacon until crisp; drain. Cube zucchini; leave the skin on. Place ingredients in skillet or saucepan. Add salt, dried basil, and chopped onion. Cook until tender.

This freezes well; as good as if you just prepared it.

Betty Pike, Pleasant Valley Baptist Church, Wichita, Kansas

SWEET POTATOES WITH BROWN SUGAR AND APRICOT SAUCE

1 cup packed brown sugar
1 cup apricot nectar
1/4 cup butter or margarine
2 t. lemon peel, grated
1/4 t. cinnamon

Dash of nutmeg
6 medium sweet potatoes,
   cooked, peeled, and cut into
   1'' slices
1/2 cup pecan halves

In medium saucepan bring sugar, nectar, butter, lemon peel, cinnamon, and nutmeg to boil. Boil gently 2 minutes. Arrange potatoes in 12''x8''x2'' baking dish. Pour sauce over potatoes. Sprinkle with pecans. Bake in preheated 350°F. oven, turning occasionally, for 30 minutes or until potatoes are heated through and sauce is bubbly. Makes 10 servings.

Linda Phillips, First Brethren Church, Peru, Indiana

SWEET POTATO CASSEROLE

3 cups sweet potatoes, cooked
   and mashed
1 cup sugar
1/2 cup milk or egg nog,
   when available
1/4 cup butter or margarine,
   melted
2 eggs, beaten

1 t. vanilla
1 cup flaked coconut (optional)
1 cup brown sugar, firmly
   packed
1/3 cup flour
1/3 cup butter or margarine,
   melted
1 cup pecans, chopped

Combine sweet potatoes, sugar, milk, butter, eggs, and vanilla; mix well. Spoon into a lightly greased 2-quart casserole. Combine coconut, brown sugar, flour, 1/3 cup melted butter, and pecans; mix well. Sprinkle over top of sweet potatoes. Bake at 375°F. for 45 minutes or until golden brown. Makes 10 servings.

Margaret Bondurant, Kensington Baptist Church, Memphis, Tennessee

SWISS POTATOES

2 lbs. frozen hash brown
   potatoes
1/4 lb. butter, melted
1/4 cup half-and-half cream

1/4 lb. Swiss cheese, grated
1/4 cup Parmesan cheese, grated
Salt and pepper to taste
Paprika

Lay potatoes in well-greased baking pan. Mix butter and cream; pour over potatoes. Sprinkle on salt and pepper to taste. Bake at 350°F. for approximately 25 minutes. Remove from oven and sprinkle cheeses on top. Return to oven until cheese bubbles and is golden brown. Sprinkle with paprika. Makes 10 servings.

Joan and Gary Phillips, Sunbury Church of Christ, Sunbury, Ohio

CHEESE POTATOES

1—2 lb. pkg. frozen hash
   browns

1 lb. Velveeta cheese, grated
1 pt. Hellman's Mayonnaise

Mix ingredients together and bake in a 13''x9'' dish at 350°F. for 30–40 minutes. Delicious.

Ann Blake, Grace United Methodist Church, Washington C.H., Ohio

COTTAGE BAKED POTATOES

4 medium–large potatoes,
   peeled and cooked
1 cup small curd cottage cheese,
   cream style
1 egg

1 t. salt
1/8 t. pepper
2 T. parsley, chopped
1 T. butter
Paprika

Combine potatoes (slightly cooled), cottage cheese, eggs, salt, and pepper. Beat with electric mixer until blended. Stir in parsley. Pile into greased 1-1/2–quart casserole. Dot top with butter; sprinkle with paprika. Bake uncovered at 350°F. for 35 minutes.

May be made ahead of time and refrigerated. Allow extra baking time.

Betty J. Warford, Central United Methodist Church, Oblong, Illinois

SCALLOPED GOURMET POTATOES

6 medium potatoes
2 cups cheddar cheese,
    shredded (Kraft's Cracker
    Barrel mild)
1/4 cup butter
1-1/2 cups sour cream

1/3 cup green onions,
    finely chopped
1 t. salt
1/4 t. pepper
2 T. butter
Paprika

Cook potatoes in skins and cool. Peel and shred coarsely. In a saucepan over low heat combine cheese and 1/4 cup butter. Stir until blended. Remove from heat and add sour cream, onions, and seasonings. Fold in potatoes and put in 2-quart casserole. Dot with 2 tablespoons butter and sprinkle with paprika. Bake uncovered at 350°F. for 30 minutes or until heated through. Makes 8 servings.

Mrs. Henrietta Kidwell, First Baptist Church, Portland, Indiana

MRS. SWEENEY'S RICE

2 cups rice
2 cans beef consomme'
1/4 cup butter
4 green onions

6–8 medium–large mushrooms
    or 1 can mushrooms
1 t. oregano

Melt butter in frying pan. Add sliced onions. Lightly saute'. In casserole dish, combine all ingredients. Bake at 350°F. for 1 hour.

The easiest, quickest thing in the world to make, but tastes great! People think Jill has fussed over the dish, and she never takes any home.

Jill Miller, Bethel Temple, San Francisco, California

JALAPEÑO RICE

2 cups Minute Rice
4 cups water
4 chicken bouillon cubes
1/2 lb. Velveeta cheese, cubed

1/2 stick margarine
1/2 cup oil
3 jalapeños, diced without seeds

Dissolve chicken bouillon cubes in boiling water. Add Minute Rice and cook slowly, uncovered, about 15 minutes. Next add cheese, oil, and margarine; cook slowly another 15 minutes, uncovered, stirring often. Last, add jalapeños and cook a little longer until very thick. Makes 8 or more servings.

Guaranteed to be creamy and spicy hot!

Lolly Burns, First Baptist Church, Combes, Texas

CHEESE GRITS

2 cups grits, cooked
    (3/4 cup grits; 3-1/2 cups
    water)
1 stick margarine, melted
1—6 oz. pkg. Kraft garlic cheese, grated

1—6 oz. pkg. Kraft jalapeño
    cheese, grated
2 t. seasoned salt
3 eggs, well beaten

Cook grits and add remaining ingredients in above order. Bake in 10''
Corning Ware skillet. Bake at 325°F. for 1 hour.

Betty G. Romine, First Baptist Church, Lake Jackson, Texas

SWEET DILL PICKLES

1 qt. dill pickles, drained and
    sliced thin
1 onion, cut fine

2 cups white sugar
3 T. cider vinegar
1/2 t. celery salt

Mix all together and let set in refrigerator for at least 24 hours before
using.

Dolores M. White, Trinity United Methodist Church, Bowling Green, Ohio

JUNE DIXON'S REFRIGERATOR PICKLES

2 qts. sliced cucumbers
2 T. pickling salt

Sugar
Vinegar

Mix and let stand 2 hours. Drain liquid. Cover with equal parts sugar
and white vinegar. Cover, but don't seal. These can be eaten in a few
hours or kept in refrigerator all winter.

Mary Anne Daily, Arthur United Methodist Church, Arthur, Illinois

LESLIE'S LIMAS

1 pkg. frozen baby lima beans
1/4 lb. mushrooms, sliced
1/4 cup onion, chopped
   (1/2 small onion)
3–4 T. butter

1 cup cabbage, finely shredded
1/2 t. salt
1 T. soy sauce
1 T. Parmesan cheese,
   freshly grated

Cook and drain limas. Sauté mushrooms and onions in butter until soft. Mix cabbage, salt, and soy sauce with mushrooms and onions, then combine with limas. Turn into a shallow 1-quart casserole. Sprinkle with cheese. Bake uncovered at 350°F. for 15–20 minutes. Serves 6. Tastes good cold for lunch the next day, too.

Leslie Wilson, La Mesa Community Church, Santa Barbara, California

BAKED PINEAPPLE

4 eggs
1 cup sugar
1/4 lb. butter or margarine

1—1lb. 4 oz. can crushed
   pineapple, drained
5 slices bread, cubed in 1'' cubes

Mix all together and bake in a greased 2-quart casserole at 350°F. for 1 hour.

This can be served with ham or as a dessert with whipped cream.

Rev. Martin W. Bovee, First Baptist Church, Red Bank, New Jersey

Pies
and
Puddings

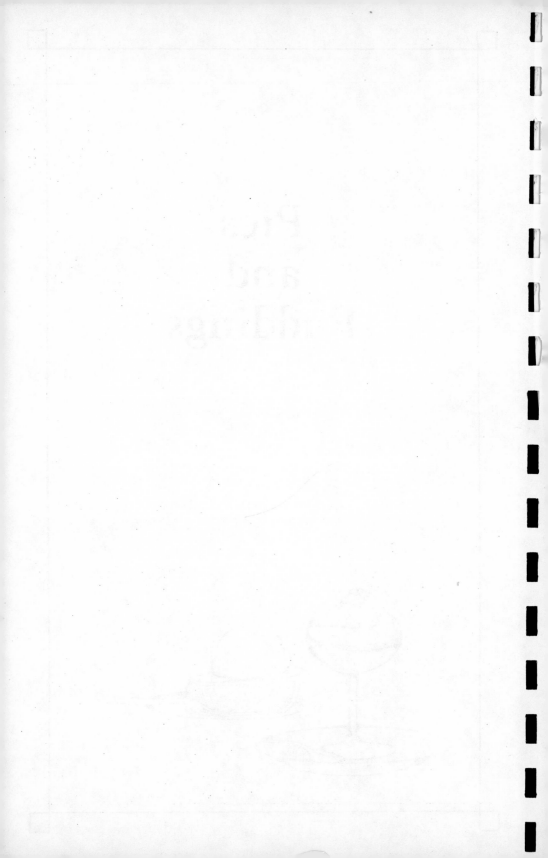

PIES

OLD TIME BUTTERMILK PIE

9'' pie shell, unbaked
1/2 cup butter
2 cups sugar
3 rounded T. flour

3 eggs, beaten
1 cup fresh buttermilk
1 t. vanilla
Dash nutmeg (optional)

Have butter soft; add sugar. Cream together well with flour. Add eggs, beat well. Stir in buttermilk, vanilla, and nutmeg. Pour into unbaked pie shell. Bake at 350°F. for 45–50 minutes.

This is a never fail recipe if the oven temperature remains at 350°F. constantly.

Mrs. Lessie Mierzwik, Memorial Baptist Church, Killeen, Texas

GRANDMA'S CUSTARD PIE

6 cups milk, scalded
6 extra large egg yolks
2 cups sugar
1 pinch salt

4 T. butter
1-1/2 t. vanilla
1/2 cup cornstarch

Mix egg yolks, sugar, salt, and cornstarch. Add *slowly* to scalded milk, stirring constantly to keep smooth until thickened. Remove from fire. Add vanilla and butter. Pour into 2 baked pie shells. Chill.

Sharon A. Weaver, Mt. Hope Community Church, Penn Hills, Pennsylvania

PAT LATHROP'S FRENCH COCONUT PIE

1 pie shell, unbaked
1 stick margarine
3 eggs

1-1/4 cups sugar
1 t. vanilla
1 can coconut

Melt margarine and beat with eggs. Add sugar and beat until well blended. Add vanilla and coconut and stir. Pour into crust and bake at 350°F. for about 50 minutes. Pie is done when it quits shaking in the middle.

Marilyn Simmons, First Baptist Church, Patterson, Louisiana

COCONUT CREAM PIE

1/2 cup sugar	3 eggs
5 rounded T. flour	1-1/2 cups milk
1/8 t. salt	1 t. vanilla
1/4 cup milk	1/2 cup coconut

Scald 1-1/2 cups milk. Mix together sugar, flour, and salt. Add 1/4 cup milk to the sugar, flour, and salt mixture. Stir this into scalded milk. Cook until thick. Beat egg yolks and add to cooked custard and cook for 2 minutes. Add vanilla and coconut. Cool and put into a baked pie shell.

MERINGUE

3 egg whites	6 T. sugar
1/4 t. cream of tartar	

Beat egg whites and tartar until stiff, but not dry. Add sugar, one tablespoon at a time. Beat until all sugar is dissolved. Put on top of the coconut cream mixture and lightly brown in oven.

Betty Hussong, First Friends Church, Marion, Indiana

CHOCOLATE RAISIN PIE

1/3 cup chocolate chips	3/4 cup sugar
1-1/2 cups raisins	1/8 t. salt
1 cup light cream	1/8 t. cinnamon
1/4 cup butter	2 eggs
3 T. cornstarch	9'' pie shell, unbaked
1 t. vanilla	

Place chocolate chips, raisins, cream, and butter in heavy saucepan. Stir over low heat until chips and butter are melted. Remove from heat and stir in vanilla. Mix together sugar, cornstarch, salt, and cinnamon. Stir into raisin mixture. Beat eggs well until foamy and stir in. Pour into unbaked pie shell spreading raisins evenly over bottom. Bake in moderate oven, 375°F., for 40–45 minutes, or until set. Cool. Top with whipped cream if desired.

Mrs. Kerri Rein, Immanuel Lutheran Church, Chadron, Nebraska

FRENCH SILK PIE

1 cup butter or margarine
1-1/2 cups sugar
2 squares unsweetened chocolate, melted

2 t. vanilla
4 eggs

Cream well butter and sugar. Blend in melted chocolate and vanilla. Add eggs 2 at a time, beating 5 minutes after each 2 eggs. Place mixture in baked 9'' pie shell. Chill 1–2 hours. Top with whipped cream and nuts.

Elda L. Saunders, Cornelius Christian Church, Cornelius, Oregon

CHOCOLATE CHIP PIE

1—6 oz. pkg. chocolate chips
3 T. milk
2 T. sugar

4 egg yolks
4 egg whites, beaten until stiff
1 t. vanilla

Melt first 3 ingredients together over hot water; cool. Add egg yolks singly, beating in each one. Add vanilla with last one. Fold stiffly beaten whites into mixture. Pour into baked, chilled crust. Chill several hours; serve with whipped cream garnish.

Doris Gilbert, First Congregational Church, Oroville, California

HEATH PIE

6 Heath candy bars
1—8-1/2 oz. pkg. Cool Whip

1 cup Nestle's Quick chocolate drink mix

Crush Heath bars in blender. Save some crumbs for top. Mix remaining ingredients with Heath crumbs. Put in prepared pie crust.

CRUST

1 cup flour
2 T. water

1 cup pecans, chopped
1 stick (1/2 cup) margarine

Blend together with pastry blender and press into pie pan. Bake at 350°F. for 20 minutes. Cool and fill.

Lou Ann McGuire, First Baptist Church, Crescent, Oklahoma

FRENCH STRAWBERRY PIE

GLAZE MIXTURE

4 cups fresh strawberries,
  washed and hulled
3/4 cup water
1/3 cup honey

Dash salt
2 T. cornstarch
1-1/2 T. water (approximately)

Pick out 2 cups of best berries and set aside. Place remaining berries in saucepan and chop. All 3/4 cup water, honey, and salt. Bring to a boil and boil hard for 2 minutes. Strain. Make a paste with cornstarch and water; add to strained juice. Return to heat and cook until thickened. Set aside to cool slightly.

CREAM MIXTURE

3 oz. cream cheese
1 T. honey
2 t. lemon juice

1/2 t. vanilla
Dash salt
1 cup whipped cream

Mix all ingredients together. Turn into 9'' baked pie shell. Place 2 cups of reserved strawberries on top of cream cheese mixture. Pour cooled glaze carefully over berries. Garnish with 1 cup whipped cream.

Sue Ann Harmon, St. Mary Church, Louisville, Kentucky

FROZEN STRAWBERRY PIE

2-1/2 cups flaked coconut,
  toasted
1/3 cup margarine, melted
1—3 oz. pkg. cream cheese,
  softened
1—14 oz. can condensed milk
  (do *not* use evaporated milk)

2-1/2 cups fresh or frozen
  strawberries, mashed or
  puréed
3 T. lemon juice from
  concentrate
1 cup (1/2 pt.) whipping cream

Combine coconut and margarine; press firmly on bottom and up side of a 9'' pie plate. In large mixing bowl, beat cheese until fluffy; gradually beat in condensed milk. Stir in puréed strawberries and lemon juice. Fold in whipped cream. Pour into prepared crust. Freeze 4 hours or until firm. Before serving, garnish with fresh strawberries, if desired. Keep leftovers in freezer.

You may use a baked 9'' pastry shell instead of coconut shell.

Mrs. Lester Stock, Pilgrim Evangelical Lutheran Church, Wauwatosa, Wisconsin

FRESH STRAWBERRY CHEESECAKE PIE

1—9'' pie shell, baked and
  cooled
1—8 oz. pkg. cream cheese
1 cup cold milk

1—3-3/4 oz. pkg. vanilla
  instant pudding
1—8 oz. container sour cream

Cream the cream cheese. Slowly add the sour cream until blended. Then add the milk and pudding; mix together until smooth. Pour into the pie shell and chill. Add topping.

TOPPING

1/2 cup sugar
1/2 cup water
1-1/2 T. cornstarch

1-1/2 T. lemon gelatin
1 small box (2 cups) fresh
  strawberries

Prepare topping by heating to a boil the sugar, water, and cornstarch. Remove from heat and add the lemon gelatin, stirring until dissolved. Cool this topping and mix together with the sliced strawberries and spoon on top of the cooled filling.

You may substitute fresh raspberries, blueberries, or peaches in the topping for a delicious change.

Sally Ohlsen, Monroe Community Chapel, Monroe, Washington

CONGEALED PEACH PIE

4 T. peach gelatin
3/4 cup water
1 small can peaches, drained

3/4 cup sugar
2 T. flour
Cool Whip

Mix gelatin, sugar, and flour. Add water. Cook until thick. Pour over fruit in graham cracker crust. Cool. Spread Cool Whip on top before serving.

Can be used with any flavor gelatin and fruit. Fruit may be fresh, frozen, or canned.

Magnolia Edwards, Southside Baptist Church, Greenville, Alabama

TRAVERSE CITY, MICHIGAN CHERRY PIE

Pastry for 8'' or 9'' pie
(for 9'' pie, increase all
ingredients by one-quarter)
3 cups tart cherries, pitted
1/8 t. salt

1 cup sugar
1/2 cup flour
4 drops almond extract
1-1/2 T. butter

Mix cherries with sugar, flour, almond extract, and salt. Pour into shell. Dot with butter. Place lattice top on, sealing with water and crimping edges high. Bake at 425 °F. for 10 minutes. Reduce heat to 350 °F. and bake another 30 minutes.

Mabel M. Philpott, Court Street United Methodist Church, Flint, Michigan

SOUR CREAM APPLE PIE

2 eggs
1-1/3 cups sugar
1/4 cup flour
1-1/3 t. vanilla

1/2 pt. buttermilk
1/8 t. yellow food coloring
1-1/2 cups chopped apples,
canned or cooked

Beat eggs and add other ingredients. Pour into unbaked pie shell and bake at 375 °F. until pie has become somewhat firm. Remove from oven and cover with topping. Return to oven for 10 minutes.

TOPPING

1/2 cup sugar
1-1/2 t. cinnamon
1/4 cup flour

1/2 stick margarine, melted
1/2 t. salt

Combine and sprinkle on top of pie.

Mary Foushee, Durham Memorial Baptist Church, Durham, North Carolina

NO-CRUST APPLE PIE

4 cooking apples
1/2 cup dry oatmeal
1T. coconut
2 T. almonds

1 T. wheat germ
2 T. brown sugar
1 t. cinnamon
2 T. butter, melted

Melt butter. Measure out other ingredients, except apples, into a medium size mixing bowl. Pour butter over mixture and stir to blend. Peel and slice apples into a 9'' pie plate. Sprinkle coarse mixture over apples and bake at 375 °F. for 25 minutes. Serves 6. Add a dollop of cream or yogurt on top when serving, if desired.

Anne Macoskie, Faith Presbyterian Church, Aurora, Colorado

APPLE PIE

PASTRY

2 cups all-purpose flour	2/3 cup shortening
1 t. salt	5–6 T. water

Mix together flour and salt. Cut in 1/3 cup shortening until the mixture has the texture of fine cornmeal. Cut in remaining shortening until particles are the size of small peas. Add water gradually, mixing with a fork until mixture forms a ball. Cover dough and refrigerate while preparing filling.

FILLING

6 cups sliced apples	1 t. lemon peel, grated
(6–8 medium apples)	1 t. ground cinnamon
3/4 cup sugar	1/4 t. ground nutmeg
2 T. flour	2 T. butter or margarine

Pare and core apples and slice thin; place in large bowl. Combine sugar, flour, lemon rind, cinnamon, and nutmeg in a small bowl. Sprinkle flour mixture over apples and toss gently until all apples are covered.

Preheat oven to 400°F. Divide pastry dough in half. Cover unused portion. Roll out half of dough on lightly floured board. Fit into 9" pie pan. Fill with apple mixture. Dot with butter. Roll out remaining half of dough and fit over pie. Seal edges. Slit top of crust. Bake at 400°F. for 55–60 minutes.

Althea Nalley, St. Mary Church, Louisville, Kentucky

OUT-OF-THIS-WORLD PIE

This makes a nice February–Valentine dessert.

1 can cherry pie filling	1—3 oz. box cherry gelatin, dry
1 large can crushed pineapple	4 bananas, sliced
with juice	1 cup pecans, chopped (optional)
1/2 cup sugar	2 baked pie shells
1 T. cornstarch	Whipped topping

In a saucepan combine cherry pie filling, sugar, pineapple and juice, and cornstarch. Cook until thick. Remove from heat and add dry gelatin. Allow to cool. Add bananas and pecans. Pour into 2 baked pie shells and top with whipped topping. Chill.

Many times Aroene makes this dessert without putting it into pie shells. It's nice in a large glass bowl, spooning it into individual parfait glasses, alternating the cherry mixture with the whipped cream.

Aroene M. Gerhab, Christ Lutheran Church, Hellertown, Pennsylvania

RASPBERRY MARSHMALLOW PIE

1 envelope unflavored gelatin
1/2 cup cold water
3/4 cup sugar
1 t. lemon juice
2 cups mini marshmallows
1—10 oz. pkg. frozen raspberries, thawed

1—8 oz. pkg. cream cheese, softened
1/2 cup heavy cream, whipped
1—9'' graham cracker crust, chilled

Soften gelatin in cold water; stir over low heat until dissolved. Cool. Crush raspberries; stir in sugar, lemon juice, and gelatin. Gradually add to softened cream cheese; mix until well blended. Chill until slightly thickened; fold in whipped cream and marshmallows. Pour into pie crust; chill until firm.

Marybeth Leonard, Glad Tidings Assembly of God, Clearfield, Pennsylvania

MILE HIGH PIE

1—10'' pie shell
2 egg whites
1/8 t. salt
1 T. lemon juice
1 cup granulated sugar

1—10 oz. pkg. frozen raspberries or strawberries
2/3 cup whipping cream
1 t. vanilla

In a very large bowl, beat egg whites, salt, lemon juice, and sugar for **20 minutes;** fold in fruit. Beat whipping cream until stiff; add vanilla. Fold cream into fruit mixture. Pour into baked 10'' pie shell. Freeze and serve frozen.

Mrs. Robert B. Selvin, First Congregational Church, Hopkinton, New Hampshire

RHUBARB CUSTARD PIE

3 cups rhubarb, cut in
  small pieces
2 T. flour
2-1/2 T. water

2 egg yolks
1 t. lemon extract
1 pie crust, unbaked
1 cup sugar

Put rhubarb in the unbaked pie shell. Beat egg yolks until light. Mix sugar and flour together and add with water to egg yolks. Beat well and flavor with lemon extract. Pour custard over rhubarb. Bake at 350°F. for about 1 hour or until done. When baked, top with meringue and brown in 350°F. oven.

MERINGUE

2 egg whites   4 T. sugar

Beat ingredients together.

This was one of Eleanor's mother's recipes, and is delicious.

Mrs. Eleanor M. Tweito, Redeemer Lutheran Church, Marshall, Missouri

PINK GRAPEFRUIT MERINGUE PIE

1—9'' pie shell, baked
6 T. cornstarch
1-1/4 cups sugar
1/4 t. salt
2 cups fresh grapefruit juice

1/2 cup cold water
3 eggs, separated
1 t. butter
1—2 drops red food coloring

Mix sugar, cornstarch, and salt together. Add grapefruit juice and water; mix thoroughly. Cook over low heat until slightly thick, then pour a little of the filling over beaten egg yolks; return to pan and cook for about 5 minutes more or until thick and clear. Remove from heat; add butter and food coloring. Cool and put into pie shell. Cover with meringue and bake in a 350°F. oven for 10–12 minutes until golden brown.

MERINGUE

3 egg whites
1/4 t. cream of tartar
1/4 t. salt

1/2 t. vanilla
6 T. sugar

Beat ingredients together.

Margaret Butler, Messiah Lutheran Church, North Ft. Myers, Florida

MISSISSIPPI LEMON CHESS PIE

2 cups sugar
1 T. all-purpose flour
1 T. cornmeal
1/4 t. salt
1/4 cup butter or margarine,
    melted (4 T. full)

1/4 cup lemon juice
Grated rind of 2 lemons
    (2 T. full)
1/4 cup milk
4 eggs
1—9'' pastry shell, unbaked

Combine sugar, flour, cornmeal, and salt. Add butter, lemon juice, lemon rind, and milk; mix well. Add eggs one at a time, beating well after each addition. Pour into pastry shell. Bake at 350°F. for 50 minutes. Makes one 9'' pie.

Cora B. Savidge, Broad Street United Methodist Church, Portsmouth, Virginia

LEMONADE PIE

2 cans Eagle Brand milk
1—12 oz. can frozen lemonade,
    not thawed

1—9 oz. container Cool Whip
3 graham cracker crusts

Put milk and frozen lemonade in a bowl and stir. Stir in the Cool Whip and mix well. Pour into graham cracker crusts.

Barbara Inabnit, Bethany Baptist Church, Snellville, Georgia

DELICIOUS PIE

1 large can crushed pineapple, drained
1 cup cherries, chopped and drained
1 cup pecans, chopped
1 large container Cool Whip
1 can condensed milk
5–6 T. lemon juice
2—9'' pie shells, baked

Slightly whip Cool Whip and condensed milk. Add lemon juice and mix well. Add nuts, cherries, and pineapple. Put in 2 baked shells. Place in refrigerator to chill. Ready to cut in about 1 hour.

Julia H. Thompson, Brookwood Baptist Church, Prichard, Alabama

PINEAPPLE MERINGUE PIE

1—1 lb. can crushed pineapple
3/4 cup sugar
2 T. flour
1/8 t. salt
1 cup dairy sour cream
3 egg yolks
1 T. lemon juice
1 pie crust, baked

Drain pineapple, reserving syrup. Combine sugar, flour, and salt in medium saucepan. Stir in crushed pineapple and then reserved syrup, sour cream, egg yolks, and lemon juice. Cook over medium heat, stirring constantly until mixture is thick. Cover and cool to lukewarm. Pour into baked crust and top with meringue. Brown at 325°F.

Grace Godwin, Fairview Cumberland Presbyterian Church, Marshall, Texas

SOUTHERN CHESS PIE

1-2/3 cups sugar
2 T. flour
2 T. cornmeal
3 eggs, beaten well
1 stick butter or margarine, melted
1 t. vanilla
1 small can pineapple
1 small can coconut

Mix above ingredients well. Pour into unbaked pie shell and bake at 435°F. for 5 minutes. Reduce to 350°F. and bake for 45 minutes.

Mrs. Billie Ray (Mary) Berry, Laurel Heights Baptist Church, Winnfield, Louisiana

JIFFY PIE

1 stick butter
1 cup flour
1 cup sugar
2 t. baking powder
2/3 cup milk
3–3-1/2 cups fruit

Melt butter in ovenproof skillet. Mix together flour, sugar, baking powder, and milk. Spoon into skillet. Do not mix with butter. Add fruit. Bake at 350°F. for 30–35 minutes.

Mrs. Amy Myers, Eastminster Presbyterian Church, Knoxville, Tennessee

PARSON'S PECAN PIE

3 whole eggs
1 cup white sugar
1 T. flour
1 cup dark Karo syrup

1 t. vanilla
1 cup pecans
Pie crust in pan

Beat eggs and sugar together until well mixed. Add flour and beat 1 minute. Add dark syrup, vanilla, and pecans. Bake in slow oven 300°F. for 1 hour until knife inserted in center comes out clean.

The slow oven will give the filling a good caramel taste and toast the pecans. A great pie.

Rev. William S. Couvillion, Lissie United Methodist Church, Lissie, Texas

MOM'S PEANUT BUTTER PIE

1—9'' crumb crust, baked
1 qt. vanilla ice cream
2/3 cup crunchy peanut butter

1 small container whipped topping (Cool Whip)

Bake and cool crust. Blend softened ice cream, peanut butter, and thawed topping. Spoon into crust. Cover with plastic wrap; freeze until solid. Let stand 5 minutes for easier cutting. Serve with chocolate sauce.

Muriel Wolfe, Grandview Presbyterian Church, Glendale, California

PEANUT BUTTER PIE

1—8 oz. pkg. cream cheese
1 cup powdered sugar
1/2 cup peanut butter

1/2 cup milk
9 oz. whipped topping

Mix together cream cheese, peanut butter, and powdered sugar. Add milk and beat again. Put into a baked 9'' pie shell. Cover with whipped topping. You may sprinkle a few chopped peanuts on top.

Marie Darling, Church of the Straits, Mackinaw City, Michigan

PEANUT BUTTER CHIFFON PIE

1 graham cracker crust
1 envelope unflavored gelatin
1/4 cup sugar
1/4 t. salt
1 cup milk

1/2 cup creamy peanut butter
2 eggs, separated
1/4 cup brown sugar
1 cup marshmallow creme
1 cup whipped topping

Combine gelatin, sugar, and salt in saucepan. Add milk, slightly beaten egg yolks, and peanut butter. Cook, stirring constantly, over medium heat. Chill until slightly thick. Add melted marshmallow creme, brown sugar, and whipped topping. Fold into peanut butter mixture. Pour into crust. Chill until firm, overnight. Add favorite topping. Makes 1 pie.

Dana Baker, Calvary Baptist Church, Connersville, Indiana

PIE CRUST

4 cups flour
1 T. sugar
2 t. salt
1-3/4 cups shortening

1 T. vinegar
1 large egg
1/2 cup water

Put first 3 ingredients in large bowl and mix well. Add shortening and mix until crumbly. In small bowl beat together water, vinegar, and egg. Combine mixtures and stir with fork until moist. Divide in 5 equal parts and chill (chilling is optional).

Marjorie Herring, Burlington Baptist Church, Omaha, Arkansas

REDI-MIX PIE CRUST

1 lb. lard
6 cups flour

2 t. salt

Mix with pastry blender or cut with 2 table knives until the consistency of peas in cornmeal. Keep refrigerated. 3 cups mix makes 2 thick crusts. Add 4 tablespoons ice water or enough so dough sticks together and can be easily rolled.

Julia Meltvedt, Church of the Straits, Mackinaw City, Michigan

HAWAIIAN APPLE PIE

1-1/2 cups crushed pineapple, drained
1 cup unsweetened applesauce
1/2 cup sugar

1/8 t. salt
1 T. cornstarch
1 T. butter
2 egg yolks, well beaten

Mix together fruits, sugar, salt, and cornstarch. Cook over direct heat for 10 minutes, stirring frequently. Gradually stir in well beaten eggs and butter. Cook 2 minutes, stirring constantly. Turn into a pre-baked pastry shell. Top with meringue and bake until lightly browned.

MERINGUE

3 egg whites
1/8 t. salt

2 T. powdered sugar

Beat until egg whites form peaks, add salt and sugar.

Zelma L. Tyler, St. Mary Church, Louisville, Kentucky

GRANDMOTHER'S DREAM PIE

Zuetta's grandmother always made Dream Pie at holidays.

3 eggs
1 cup sugar
1 T. vinegar
1-1/2 T. margarine, melted
1 t. flour

1/2 t. allspice
1/2 t. nutmeg
1/2 cup raisins
1/2 cup pecans, broken

Beat eggs in bowl. Add other ingredients and bake in unbaked 9'' pie crust at 350°F. until silver knife comes out clean.

Zuetta Putty, Eastern Heights Church, Cleburne, Texas

PUDDINGS

MAINE INDIAN PUDDING

1/3 cup cornmeal
1 qt. milk
1–1-1/2 t. ginger

1/2 cup molasses
1 t. salt

Warm milk and pour it over rest of ingredients in a bowl. Cook 1–1-1/2 hours in a double boiler, stirring occasionally. Serve with cream, whipped cream, or ice cream.

Frances Carpenter, Trinity Baptist Church, Lynnfield, Massachusetts

DATE PUDDING

1-1/2 cups dates
1-1/2 cups water
1 t. baking soda
1 cup sugar
1/4 cup butter
1 egg, beaten
2 cups flour
1 t. baking powder

1/2 t. salt
1 t. vanilla
1 cup sugar
1 cup dates
Pinch of salt
3/4 cup water
1/2 cup nuts
1/4 cup maraschino cherries

Bring first 2 ingredients to a boil. Add baking soda to this while hot. Cream together sugar, butter, and egg. Add date mixture to this. Add flour, baking powder, salt, and vanilla. Mix well. Put in greased and floured 9''x13'' pan. Bake at 350°F. for 30 minutes.

Prepare the following while the cake is baking: Boil 1 cup sugar, 3/4 cup water, and 1 cup dates until mixture thickens. Add nuts, pinch of salt, and chopped maraschino cherries. Spread this on top of hot cake. Serve warm or cold with whipped topping.

Mrs. George A. Krengel, Zion Lutheran Church, Ogden, Iowa

HOT FUDGE PUDDING

1-1/2 cups Bisquick
1/2 cup sugar
1/2 cup nuts, chopped
1/2 cup milk

1/2 cup brown sugar, packed
1-1/2 cups boiling water
1—6 oz. pkg. semi-sweet
   chocolate bits

Heat oven to 350°F. Mix Bisquick, sugar, nuts, and milk. Turn batter into greased 2-quart baking dish. Sprinkle with brown sugar. Pour water over chocolate bits. Let stand 1–2 minutes until chocolate melts, then stir until blended; pour over batter. Bake 40–45 minutes. Let stand 5 minutes to cool slightly.

During baking, the pudding will rise to the top of the dish and the sauce will form at the bottom. Invert servings on plates; dip sauce over each. Serve with cream. You may substitute butterscotch bits for chocolate.

Linda Metzgar, Dunmore Presbyterian Church, Dunmore, Pennsylvania

SWEET/SOUR PUDDING

1/2 pt. sour cream
1 can chunk pineapple, drained
1 can mandarin oranges, cut up

1 cup miniature marshmallows
1/2 cup maraschino cherries,
   cut up

Combine all ingredients together. Let stand in tight container at least 12 hours in refrigerator. Serve with delicate cookies for a hot summer day treat.

Mrs. Richard I. Gourley, First Congregational Church, Hopkinton, New Hampshire

STRAWBERRY PUDDING DESSERT

1/2 large angel food cake
1—3 oz. pkg. instant vanilla
    pudding
1 cup milk
1 pt. vanilla ice cream, softened
1 pkg. strawberry gelatin

1 cup hot water
1—8 oz. pkg. frozen
    strawberries
1 container whipped topping
    (Cool Whip)

Break angel food cake into bite-size pieces. Put into 11-1/2''x7-1/2''x 1-1/2'' baking dish. Beat instant vanilla pudding with milk. Stir in softened ice cream; pour over cake. Set in refrigerator until firm, about 10 minutes. Mix gelatin with hot water. Add thawed strawberries; pour over cake mixture. Let stand in refrigerator until firm. Frost with whipped topping.

Iris Poole, Trinity Methodist Church, West Frankfort, Illinois

BANANA PUDDING

3 boxes instant vanilla pudding
    mix
5 cups milk
2 boxes vanilla wafers

1—8 oz. sour cream
1—12 oz. container Cool Whip
7 bananas

Mix instant pudding and milk until thick. Fold in sour cream and Cool Whip. Put alternate layers of wafers, bananas, and pudding mixture in casserole dish. Make day before serving.

Magnolia Edwards, Butler Baptist Association, Greenville, Alabama

DORIS CREASER'S LEMON PUDDING SALAD

Served at Rescue Mission on Thanksgiving.

1 pkg. lemon pudding or
    1 can lemon pudding
1 cup whipped topping or
    whipping cream

1 can mandarin oranges
1 can pineapple tidbits
1 can fruit cocktail
1–2 bananas

Cook pudding. Cool. Fold in whipped topping. Drain fruit, fold in. Can be made day before and is good for picnics as it doesn't soften.

Maxine Pihlaja, American Lutheran Church, Billings, Montana

BREAD PUDDING

4 cups milk
1/2 t. salt
4 T. cornstarch
2 t. vanilla
1 cup sugar

4 eggs, separated (3 egg yolks and 1 whole egg, well beaten)
3 pieces of toast, cut in small cubes

Mix sugar, salt, and cornstarch. Add 1/4 cup milk to form a paste. Bring milk to boiling point. Add paste mixture and 1 egg plus 3 yolks, which have been well beaten. Cook over low heat until it comes to a boil or of custard-like pudding. Add vanilla. Put bread in casserole and pour pudding mixture over.

Beat egg whites with 1/4 teaspoon cream of tartar. Add 6 tablespoons sugar gradually. Beat until sugar is no longer felt when meringue is rubbed between fingers. Pile meringue on pudding mixture. Put casserole in pan of hot water and bake at 400°F. for 10 minutes. Coconut or jelly may be placed on top of pudding before meringue.

Mrs. Arlene G. Pursell, Durham Lutheran Church, Durham, Pennsylvania

CHOCOLATE DELIGHT

3/4 cup butter or margarine, melted
1-1/2 cups all-purpose flour
3/4 cup pecans, finely chopped
1—8 oz. pkg. cream cheese, softened
1 cup powdered sugar

1—3-3/4 oz. pkg. instant vanilla pudding mix
1—4-1/2 oz. pkg. instant chocolate pudding mix
3 cups milk
Chopped pecans
Grated chocolate

1—13 oz. carton frozen whipped topping, thawed and divided in half

Combine butter, flour, and pecans, mixing well. Press into a 13"x9"x 2" pan. Bake at 375°F. for 15 minutes. Cool completely. Combine cream cheese, powdered sugar, and 1-1/2 cups whipped topping; blend thoroughly. Spread over crust; chill. Combine pudding mixes and milk; beat 2 minutes with rotary mixer at medium speed. Spread over cream cheese layer. Spread remaining whipped topping over pudding layer. Garnish with pecans and chocolate. Refrigerate. Makes about 15 servings.

May use different pudding flavors if desired. Example: Lemon Lush.

Rev. Julia Case, Resurrection Fellowship Church, Loveland, Colorado

Cakes
and
Toppings

CAKES

ITALIAN CREAM CAKE

2 cups sugar
1/2 cup butter, softened
1/2 cup shortening
5 eggs, separated
1 t. baking soda

1 cup buttermilk
2 cups flour, sifted
1 cup coconut
1 t. vanilla

Cream sugar, butter, and shortening. Add egg yolks, beating after each addition. Dissolve baking soda in buttermilk and add alternately with flour to egg mixture. Add coconut, fold in stiffly beaten egg whites; add vanilla. Pour into three 8'' greased and floured cake pans. Bake at 350°F. for 25–30 minutes. Cool and frost.

FROSTING

1/2 cup butter, softened
1-1/2 t. vanilla
1—8 oz. pkg. cream cheese,
  softened

1 cup pecans, chopped
1-1/2 lbs. powdered sugar,
  sifted
Milk to moisten

Mix butter and cream cheese. Add sugar, vanilla, and nuts. Moisten with milk to spreading consistency. Ice only tops of layers.

Frances Clay, Second Baptist Church, Searcy, Arkansas

VENETIA STEELE'S MOIST POUND CAKE

2 sticks margarine
1/2 cup shortening
3 cups sugar
6 eggs
3 cups cake flour

1 cup milk
1 t. vanilla
1 t. lemon
1 t. salt

Mix margarine, shortening, and sugar. Add eggs and mix. Add half of milk along with the flavorings. Add half of flour, mixing well. Add remainder of milk and flour, mixing well. Pour into a greased and floured tube pan. Bake at 325°F. for 1 hour and 25 minutes.

Debbie Phillips, Jackson Park Pentecostal Holiness Church, Kannapolis, North Carolina

GERMAN TORTE CAKE

1 lb. sweet cream butter
  (no substitutes)
1—8 oz. carton sour cream
3 cups sugar

6 eggs
3 cups flour
1/4 t. baking powder
1-1/2 t. vanilla

Cream butter (Ada melts her butter and lets it cool, as she doesn't like to cream), sugar, sour cream, and eggs. Add dry ingredients and mix with electric mixer. Add vanilla and continue mixing. Bake in a well-greased and floured angel food cake pan at 325°F. for 1 hour and 20 minutes. Cool before removing from pan.

This cake improves with taste after a few days. It also freezes well.

Ada Bess Hill, First Baptist Church, Marietta, Oklahoma

CREME DE MENTHE CAKE

1 regular white cake mix
  (no pudding added)
1/2 cup and 2 T. creme de menthe syrup

Hot fudge topping
8 oz. Cool Whip

Mix regular cake mix according to directions and add 1/2 cup creme de menthe. Bake as directed. Cool cake completely. Frost a thin layer of hot fudge topping on cool cake. Frost with Cool Whip with 2 tablespoons creme de menthe added. Refrigerate at least 12 hours before serving.

Vivian Tucker, Peace Lutheran Church, Fargo, North Dakota

RED VELVET CAKE

2 cups oil
2-1/2 cups plain flour
1-1/2 cups sugar
1 cup buttermilk
2 eggs
1 t. vanilla

1-1/2 oz. red food coloring
2 t. vinegar
2 t. cocoa
1 t. baking soda
1 t. salt

Combine all ingredients in mixing bowl and beat. Bake in layers at 350°F. about 25–35 minutes.

FROSTING

1 box powdered sugar
2—8 oz. pkgs. cream cheese
1 stick margarine

1 t. vanilla
1 cup nuts, chopped

Mix well and spread on cake.

Shirley Adams, Grace Baptist Church, Dade City, Florida

TUNNEL OF FUDGE CAKE

CAKE

1-1/2 cups butter, softened
6 eggs, room temperature
1-1/2 cups sugar
2 cups flour

1 pkg. Pillsbury Double Dutch
   Fudge Buttercream ''Rich &
   Easy'' Frosting Mix*
2 cups nuts, chopped*

Cream butter in large mixer bowl at high speed. Add eggs, one at a time, beating well after each addition. Gradually add sugar; continue creaming on high until light and fluffy. By hand stir in flour, frosting mix, and nuts until well blended. Pour batter into well-greased (not floured) bundt pan. Bake at 350°F. for 60 minutes.* Cool 2 hours* before removing from pan. Cool completely and drizzle with chocolate glaze.

*NOTE: These items are necessary for successful results. Also, bake cake the full 60 minutes; no more, no less. Let cake set 2 hours before removing from pan to allow the ''tunnel'' to set.

GLAZE

1 square unsweetened chocolate
1 T. butter
3/4 cup powdered sugar

Dash of salt
2 T. hot milk

Melt chocolate and butter over low heat in saucepan. Remove from heat and add powdered sugar and salt. Blend in milk until mixture is of glaze consistency. Drizzle over cooled cake.

Leuna Bagwell, First Baptist Church, Zeigler, Illinois

CHERRY CHOCOLATE CAKE

1 pkg. fudge chocolate cake mix
1 can cherry pie filling

1 t. almond flavoring
2 eggs, beaten

Mix by hand in large bowl first 3 ingredients. Add eggs. Pour in a 13''x15''x2'' pan. Bake 350°F. for 25–30 minutes.

ICING

2 T. butter
1 cup sugar
1—6 oz. pkg. semi-sweet chocolate pieces

1/3 cup milk

Mix butter, sugar, and milk together in pot and bring to boil. Boil 1 minute. Take off fire and stir in semi-sweet chocolate until smooth. Pour over cake (Mixture will be thin but it will harden).

Myrtle Luker, Wesley First United Methodist Church, Clute, Texas

MILKY WAY CAKE

7—2 oz. Milky Way bars
1/2 cup margarine, melted
2 cups sugar
1/2 cup margarine, softened
4 eggs
3 cups all-purpose flour

1 t. vanilla
1-1/2 cups buttermilk
1/2 t. baking soda
1 cup pecans, chopped
Milk chocolate frosting

Combine candy bars and 1/2 cup margarine in a saucepan. Place over low heat until candy bars are melted, stirring constantly. Cool. Cream sugar and 1/2 cup margarine until light and fluffy. Add eggs one at a time, beating well after each addition. Add vanilla. Combine buttermilk and baking soda. Add to creamed mixture alternately with flour, beating well after each addition. Stir in candy bar mixture and pecans. Pour batter into a greased and floured 10'' tube pan. Bake at 325 °F. for 1 hour and 20 minutes. Cool and then remove from pan. Frost with milk chocolate frosting.

Judy Arrowood, Deep Springs Baptist Church, Peachland, North Carolina

CHOCOLATE MOUSSE CAKE

1 pkg. prepared chocolate
   cake mix
1—7 oz. bag frozen coconut
1 cup granulated sugar

12 large marshmallows
1 cup whole milk
1 can prepared chocolate
   frosting

Prepare cake batter according to instructions on package. Bake in two 9'' cake pans, according to baking time. Cool. Split layers into 4 layers.

Heat coconut, sugar, marshmallows, and milk on medium heat until melted. Cool for 5 minutes, then spread between 3 layers. Frost with chocolate frosting.

Dollie C. Bass, Mount Pleasant Baptist Church, Gaston, South Carolina

CHOCOLATE CARAMEL CAKE

1/3 cup evaporated milk
1 pkg. German chocolate
   cake mix
3/4 cup butter, melted

1 cup nuts, chopped
1—6 oz. pkg. chocolate chips
60 Kraft caramels
1/2 cup evaporated milk

Mix 1/3 cup milk with cake mix. Add butter and nuts. Spread half of mixture in a 9''x13'' greased pan (Mixture will be thick). Bake at 350 °F. for 8 minutes. In saucepan combine chocolate chips, caramels, 1/2 cup milk and melt. Pour over warm, baked cake. Pat rest of cake mixture on top. Bake 18–20 minutes longer.

Geneva Livesay, Kensington Baptist Church, Memphis, Tennessee

OH HO CAKE

1 pkg. chocolate cake mix	1 stick margarine
1 cup milk	1/3 cup shortening
2 T. cornstarch	1 t. vanilla
1 cup sugar	

Bake cake mix on a jelly roll pan for 15–20 minutes. Cook milk and cornstarch until thick. Cool well. Combine and cream in a bowl the remaining ingredients. After creaming, combine with cooked milk; beat until smooth and creamy; put on cake.

SAUCE

1 stick and 2 T. margarine, melted	3 cups powdered sugar
	1 egg, beaten some
6 T. cocoa	1 t. vanilla
2-1/2 T. hot water	

Melt margarine in a pan. Add remaining ingredients and beat well with a spoon. Immediately pour on top of cake. It will run and then harden.

Gail Riley, Greentown United Methodist Church, Greentown, Ohio

CHOCOLATE SHEET CAKE

2 cups flour	3-1/2 T. cocoa
2 cups sugar	1 cup water
1/2 cup margarine	1/2 cup buttermilk
1/2 cup shortening	2 eggs, unbeaten
1 t. baking soda	1 t. vanilla

Mix together flour and sugar; set aside. In saucepan, mix margarine, shortening, cocoa, and water; let come to a boil. Remove from heat and pour over flour and sugar mixture and beat together. Then add buttermilk, eggs, baking soda, and vanilla. Mix together. Grease and flour an 11''x16'' sheet pan. Bake at 400°F. for 20 minutes. After cake has baked 15 minutes, prepare frosting.

FROSTING

1/2 cup margarine	1 lb. powdered sugar
3-1/2 T. cocoa	1 t. vanilla
1/3 cup milk	

Put margarine, cocoa, and milk in a saucepan and let come to a boil. Remove from heat and add powdered sugar and vanilla. Nuts are optional. Pour icing immediately over hot cake as it comes out of the oven.

For variety, put peanut butter in the icing.

Janet Tindall, Pilgrim Lutheran Church, Wauwatosa, Wisconsin

MRS. CHENEY'S NOBBY APPLE CAKE

1 cup granulated sugar	1 cup flour
1/4 cup shortening	1/2 t. baking powder
1 egg, beaten	1/2 t. baking soda
1 t. vanilla	1/2 t. salt
3 cups apples, diced	1/2 t. cinnamon
1/4 cup walnuts, chopped	1/2 t. nutmeg
(optional)	

Cream shortening and sugar. Mix flour with spices. Peel and cut apples in small 1/2'' cubes. Add beaten egg, apples, nuts, vanilla, and flour mixture to creamed sugar mixture in that order (will be very lumpy!). Bake in a greased 8'' square pan at 350°F. for 45 minutes.

May be doubled in a 9''x13'' pan. Also, freezes well. Serve hot or cold, with or without ice cream or whipped cream.

Mrs. Edward C. Leadbeater, First Congregational Church, Hopkinton, New Hampshire

HUNGARIAN APPLE CAKE (ALMAS KALAS)

1/4 lb. butter or margarine	1 t. baking powder
1 cup sugar	1/2 t. salt
2 eggs	1/2 cup milk
1 t. vanilla	6–8 apples, peeled, cored, and
2 cups flour	sliced

Cream butter and sugar; add eggs and vanilla. Mix well. Add flour, baking powder, salt, and milk. Batter will be a little thick. Spread with a spoon to cover a greased 10''x16''x1'' baking pan. Peel, core, and slice 6–8 apples, laying slices over batter. Put crumb topping over apples. Bake in a moderate oven (350°F.) for 25–30 minutes or until done. Dust with powdered sugar when cool.

This is a thin cake, but very tasty.

CRUMB TOPPING

2 cups flour	2 t. cinnamon
1-1/2 cups sugar	1/2 lb. butter

Mix together well by hand and crumble mixture over apples.

Betty Crumley, Patterson Memorial Presbyterian Church, West Orange, New Jersey

COCOA APPLE CAKE

3 eggs
2 cups sugar
1 cup margarine, softened
1/2 cup water
2-1/2 cups all-purpose flour
2 T. cocoa
1 t. baking soda
1 t. cinnamon

1 t. allspice
1 cup nuts, finely chopped
1/2 cup chocolate chips
2 apples, peeled, cored, and
  finely chopped to equal
  2 cups
1 t. vanilla

Heat oven to 325°F. Grease and flour a 10" angel food cake pan, with removable bottom. In large mixer bowl, beat eggs, sugar, margarine, and water until fluffy. Sift flour, cocoa, baking soda, cinnamon, and allspice together. Add to egg mixture and beat until thoroughly mixed. Fold in nuts, chocolate chips, apples, and vanilla. Spread batter in pan. Bake 70 minutes or until wooden pick inserted comes out clean. Cool 10 minutes and remove from pan.

Margaret Lamphier, United Methodist Church, Wells, Minnesota

MINIATURE CHERRY CHEESE CAKES

2—8 oz. pkgs. cream cheese
2 t. vanilla
2 eggs

1/2 cup sugar
1 can cherry pie filling
1 box vanilla wafer cookies

Combine cream cheese, vanilla, eggs, and sugar and beat until smooth. Place vanilla wafers in bottom of cupcake pan liners. Fill with cheese mix to 2/3 full. Bake at 350°F. for 15 minutes. Cakes will rise as they cook. When cool, the cakes will fall. When cooled, place 1 teaspoon of uncooked cherry pie filling on top. Makes approximately 40.

Mrs. Philip D. Bell, Jr., First Congregational Church, Hopkinton, New Hampshire

SLOVAK BUTTER CAKE

1/2 lb. butter
2 cups sugar
2 t. vanilla
2 cups flour

2 t. baking powder
1/3 cup water
6 eggs, separated
1 cup ground walnuts

Beat 6 egg whites stiffly and set aside. Cream butter, sugar, and vanilla. Add egg yolks and mix well. Add flour and baking powder alternately with water. Fold in stiffly beaten egg whites. Pour into an 11"x15" pan and sprinkle with ground walnuts. Bake at 350°F. for 30–40 minutes. Cut into moon shapes while warm, using circle cutter if you don't have a moon shape cake cutter (#2 size can works well). Sprinkle with powdered sugar when ready to serve.

Arlene M. Gerhab, Christ Lutheran Church, Hellertown, Pennsylvania

APRICOT LEMON DELIGHT CAKE

1 pkg. Lemon Supreme cake mix
1/2 cup sugar
1 cup apricot nectar
3/4 cup cooking oil
4 eggs
1/2 t. vanilla extract
1/2 t. lemon extract

Mix together cake mix and sugar. Make well in center and add nectar and oil; mix. Add eggs one at a time. Then add vanilla and lemon extract. Bake in a greased tube pan at 325°F. for 1 hour. With fork, put holes in cooled cake while still in pan, then spoon glaze over cake. Dot does this several times until the glaze is gone.

GLAZE

2 cups powdered sugar
Juice of 2 lemons or balance of nectar

Mix together and spoon over cake.

Dot Rowe, Campville Group Ministry, Melrose, Florida

PENNSYLVANIA DUTCH SHOOFLY CAKE

Excellent for church potlucks, bake sales, etc.

4 cups flour
2 cups brown sugar
1/4 cup margarine
1/2 cup butter or margarine
2 eggs, beaten
1-1/2 cups King molasses or
    1 cup Brier Rabbit
1 T. baking soda
2 cups boiling water

Combine flour, brown sugar, margarine, and butter in large bowl. Work together with hands to form crumbs; set aside 1 cup of crumbs for topping. In separate bowl, combine beaten eggs and molasses. Add baking soda to boiling water and combine with egg/molasses mixture. Mix dry and liquid ingredients together in bowl. Pour into a 9"x13" pan that has been sprayed with Pam. Sprinkle the reserved 1 cup of crumbs on top. Bake at 350°F. for 45–60 minutes.

A moist cake. It will keep for days and serves 16.

Joan Hostetter, Zion Evangelical Lutheran Church, Landisville, Pennsylvania

MOUND CAKE

1 pkg. devil's food cake mix
1 large can cream of coconut
1 can Eagle Brand milk

1—9 oz. container Cool Whip
1 pkg. frozen coconut

Bake cake mix as directed on package. Bake in 13''x9'' pan. Let cool 10 minutes. With utility fork, make holes all over the cake. Beat together cream of coconut and Eagle Brand milk and pour over cake while warm. When cool, top with Cool Whip and coconut.

If desired, drizzle a small amount of melted chocolate in stripes or squares on top.

Linda R. Johnson, Brick Christian Church, Watauga, Tennessee

NO FROSTING OATMEAL CAKE

1 cup oatmeal
1-1/2 cups boiling water
1 cup brown sugar
1 cup white sugar
1/2 cup shortening
2 eggs

1-1/2 cups flour
1/2 t. salt
1 t. baking soda
1 T. cocoa
1/2 cup chocolate chips

Pour boiling water over oatmeal and set aside. Cream together brown sugar, white sugar, shortening, and eggs. Sift together the flour, salt, baking soda, and cocoa. Add dry ingredients alternately with oatmeal to the creamed mixture. Add chocolate chips and mix well. Pour batter into greased and floured 8''x12'' or 9''x13'' pan and sprinkle top with 1/2 cup chopped nuts and 1/2 cup chocolate chips. Bake at 350°F. for 35–40 minutes.

Mrs. Yvonne Clyde, Smithtown Church, DuBois, Pennsylvania

BLUEBERRY CAKE

1/2 cup shortening
1 cup sugar
2 eggs
1-3/4 cups flour
2 t. baking powder

1/2 t. salt
1/2 cup milk
1 t. vanilla
1 cup fresh or frozen
  blueberries

Cream together shortening, eggs, and sugar; beat well. Add flour, baking powder, and salt alternately with milk which has vanilla added to it. Fold in blueberries. Put in greased and floured 9''x13'' pan. Bake at 350°F. for 30 minutes.

Delicious served hot.

Mrs. Peggy Farrar, South Main Street Congregational Church, Manchester, New Hampshire

GRANDMOTHER ZIEGLE'S BLITZ KUCHEN (LIGHT CAKE)

This recipe is probably over 100 years old. It is used for coffee hours and committee meetings.

1-1/2 cups sugar	2 cups flour
1/2 cup butter or margarine	2 t. baking powder
3 eggs	1/2 t. lemon
1/2 cup milk	1/2 t. vanilla

Mix well in order given. Put in greased and floured 8''x8'' pan. Sprinkle top with topping mixture. Bake at 350°F. for 20 minutes or until done.

TOPPING

1/2 cup nutmeats	1/4 cup sugar
1/4–1/2 t. cinnamon	

Mix ingredients together and sprinkle on cake batter.

Ida Klopfenstein, Eureka Presbyterian Church, Eureka, Illinois

ADA SUNDAHL'S PIG 'N' WHISTLE CAKE

Served at Circle Meetings.

2 eggs	1 t. baking powder
1 cup sugar	1 t. vanilla
1 cup flour	1/2 cup scalded milk

Beat eggs. Add rest of ingredients. Bake at 350°F. for 20–30 minutes in 9'' pan. Immediately pour topping over and return to oven until bubbling and lightly brown.

TOPPING

1/3 cup butter	1 cup nuts, chopped
5–6 T. cream	1/2 cup coconut
1 cup brown sugar	

Melt butter in saucepan. Add other ingredients. Boil 1–2 minutes. Pour over cake.

Can be doubled for 9''x13'' pan.

Maxine Pihlaja, American Lutheran Church, Billings, Montana

ORANGE ZUCCHINI BUNDT CAKE

2-1/2 cups all-purpose flour
2 t. baking powder
1 t. baking soda
1 t. salt
2 t. grated orange rind
2 t. cinnamon
1/2 t. cloves

3 eggs
1-1/3 cups sugar
1/2 cup cooking oil
1/2 cup orange juice
1-1/2 cups zucchini, shredded
   and unpeeled

Add together flour, baking powder, baking soda, salt, spices, and orange rind; set aside. Beat eggs; add sugar. Beat in oil and orange juice. Add dry ingredients alternately with zucchini. Spread in greased bundt pan. Bake at 350°F. for 50–55 minutes. Cool in pan for 10 minutes. Remove from pan and cool. Drizzle with orange glaze.

ORANGE GLAZE

1 T. milk
1 T. butter

1-1/4 cups powdered sugar
1 T. orange juice

Heat milk and butter in saucepan. Stir in sugar; add orange juice. Beat until smooth.

Beulah Glisan, Church of God, Markleysburg, Pennsylvania

TOASTED BUTTER PECAN CAKE

2 cups pecans, chopped
1-1/4 cups butter
3 cups sifted flour
4 eggs, unbeaten
2 t. vanilla

2 t. baking powder
1/2 t. salt
2 cups sugar
1 cup milk

Toast pecans in 1/4 cup butter in a 350°F. oven for 20–25 minutes. Stir often. Sift flour with baking powder and salt. Cream 1 cup butter; gradually add sugar, creaming well. Blend in eggs; beat well after each addition. Add dry ingredients alternately with milk, beginning and ending with dry ingredients. Stir in vanilla and 1-1/2 cups pecans. Turn into three greased and floured 9'' round pans. Bake at 350°F. for 25–30 minutes. Cool and frost.

FROSTING

1/4 cup butter
1 lb. box powdered sugar

1 t. vanilla
4–5 T. evaporated milk

Cream butter. Add remaining ingredients and cream until of spreading consistency. Stir in remaining pecans. Frost tops of cake only.

Pat Clay, Cloverdale Church of Christ, Searcy, Arkansas

CHERRY NUT CAKE

1/2 lb. butter or margarine
1—13 oz. can evaporated milk
2 cups sugar
2 eggs
3 cups all-purpose flour
1/2 t. salt

2 t. baking powder
1 t. vanilla extract
1 t. almond extract
1 cup walnuts, chopped
1 cup maraschino cherries,
  chopped

Beat with beater: butter, sugar, eggs, and milk. Mix together flour, baking powder, and salt. Add dry ingredients to batter. Add vanilla and almond extract. Add walnuts and cherries. Pour into greased and floured angel food (tube) pan. Bake at 350°F. about 95 minutes or until toothpick comes out clean. Let set in pan about 15–20 minutes, then take outer pan off and let cool in funnel until cold.

Bernice Bobbitt, Messiah Evangelical Lutheran Church, Chicago, Illinois

SNOWBALL CAKE

2 pkg. unflavored gelatin
1 large angel food cake
2 large containers Cool Whip
1 cup coconut, shredded
1 cup cold water

1—16 oz. can crushed pineapple
  with juice
1 cup sugar
2 T. lemon juice
1 cup hot water

Dissolve gelatin in cold water; add hot water, sugar, lemon juice, and pineapple. Chill until partially set. Add 1 container Cool Whip to gelatin. Line 9''x13'' pan with waxed paper. Pinch off pieces of cake and line pan with it. Cover with half the gelatin-fruit mixture, then another layer of cake, then rest of mixture. Mash down with back of spoon. Chill overnight. Turn out on tray and frost with second container of Cool Whip and cover with coconut.

Betty Simmons, St. Paul's United Methodist Church, Kensington, Maryland

TAHITIAN BRUNCH CAKE

1 pkg. banana cake mix
3/4 cup water
3 eggs
1—8-1/2 oz. can crushed pineapple, drained

1/4 cup pineapple liquid
1/2 cup nuts

Mix and bake in bundt cake pan at 350°F. for 25 minutes.

GLAZE

1 cup powdered sugar

3 T. liquid

Blend and pour over cake.

Frances G. Hogan, Lebanon Baptist Church, Lebanon, Kentucky

NANCY WARE'S CAKE

CAKE

1—18.5 oz. pkg. yellow   4 eggs
   cake mix   1/2 cup cooking oil
1—11 oz. can mandarin oranges with juice

Mix together all ingredients with electric mixer until orange slices are broken up and batter is fluffy (about 3 minutes). Divide among three greased and floured 9'' layer cake pans and bake at 350°F. about 20 minutes or until cake tests done. Cool on rack. When layers are cool, ice between layers, sides, and top. Makes 12–14 servings.

ICING

1—20 oz. can crushed pineapple   1—3 oz. pkg. instant vanilla
   with juice   pudding mix, uncooked
1—8 or 9 oz. container whipped topping mix

Blend ingredients; mix well. Keep refrigerated until used.

This cake must be refrigerated!

Jennie Williamson, Presbyterian Church of the Covenant, Bala Cynwyd, Pennsylvania

MIRACLE FRUIT CAKE

1 cup dates, sliced   1 lb. Dromedary fruit and peels
1 cup seedless raisins   1 cup nuts, chopped
2/3 cup margarine   3 cups flour
1-1/4 cups brown sugar, packed   1/2 t. cinnamon
1/4 cup dark molasses   1/2 t. ground nutmeg
1-1/2 cups hot water   1 t. baking powder
2 eggs   1 t. baking soda
1 t. vanilla   1 t. salt

Combine first 6 ingredients. Boil gently for 3 minutes. Cool in a large mixing bowl. Beat in eggs. Add fruit and peels and nuts. Sift remaining ingredients; add gradually to fruit mixture, beating well after each addition. Add vanilla. Pour into 9'' tube pan which has been greased and bottom covered with waxed paper. Bake at 300°F. for 2 hours or until it tests done. Let cool thoroughly before removing from pan. Wrap securely in foil or waxed paper. Store in a cool place. Age 3–4 weeks to improve flavor; 6 weeks is desirable. It's very good right away.

Mona B. Herring, Church of God, Markleysburg, Pennsylvania

SHOO-FLY CUPCAKES

2-1/2 cups flour
1-1/2 cups light brown sugar
1/2 cup butter
1 t. baking powder

1 cup light brown sugar
1-1/2 cups boiling water
1 t. baking soda

Combine first 4 ingredients and make crumbs; save 1 cup for topping. To remaining crumbs, add last 3 ingredients and mix all together by hand. Fill cups 1/2 full and sprinkle crumbs on top of each. Bake at 350°F. for 25 minutes. Makes 2 dozen.

Mrs. Linda Heiser, East Fairview Church of the Brethren, Manheim, Pennsylvania

SURPRISE CUPCAKES

1 pkg. chocolate cake mix
1—8 oz. pkg. cream cheese
1/3 cup sugar

1 egg
6 oz. chocolate chips

Prepare cake mix as directed on box. Beat together cream cheese, sugar, and egg. Add chocolate chips. Fill cupcake tins 2/3 full of batter, then drop a teaspoon of cream cheese filling in center. Bake at 350°F. for 15 minutes.

Edna L. Senoff, The Moravian Church of the Good Shepherd, New Hartford, New York

100 YEAR OLD BLACK WALNUT CAKE

1/2 lb. butter
1 cup cream or half and half
3 cups plain flour
1/2 cup shortening
5 eggs

1 t. vanilla
1 t. baking powder
3 cups sugar
3/4–1 cup black walnuts
(no substitutions)

Cream butter and shortening, then add the sugar. Add eggs, one at a time. Add vanilla and flour. Put baking powder in the cream and add to batter. Stir in the walnuts. Bake in a 325°F. oven in greased and floured tube pan for 1 hour 20 minutes.

Emmie Mayhand, St. Thomas Episcopal Church, Columbus, Georgia

TOPPINGS

HOT CHOCOLATE SAUCE
3/4 cup cocoa
3 cups sugar
1/4 lb. margarine

1 can evaporated milk
1 t. vanilla

Mix ingredients in double boiler and cook over hot water, stirring occasionally, about 20 minutes. Add vanilla and serve warm over ice cream.

Mary Ann Cording, Sunbury Church of Christ, Sunbury, Ohio

BAKERY ICING
2 egg whites, beaten
1/4 t. salt
Vanilla to taste

3-1/2 cups powdered sugar
1/2 cup shortening

Beat egg whites. Add salt, flavoring, and powdered sugar. Mix part of powdered sugar with shortening then combine with first ingredients. Beat well. Makes enough frosting for a 2-layer cake.

Loretta Fossum, Assembly of God, Williston, North Dakota

CREAM CHEESE FROSTING
1—3 oz. pkg. cream cheese
1/4 cup butter or margarine
1 t. vanilla

2 cups powdered sugar, sifted
Chopped nuts (optional)

In mixer bowl beat together cream cheese, butter or margarine, and vanilla until light and fluffy. Gradually add powdered sugar, beating until smooth. Spread frosting over cooled cake or cookies. Sprinkle with chopped nuts, if desired.

This makes enough to frost the tops of two 8'' or 9'' layers, top of one 13''x9'' cake, bar cookies, or about 18 cupcakes. Store, covered, in refrigerator.

Deloris Heminger, First United Methodist Church, Wood River, Nebraska

HOPELESS TWINKY FILLING

1 cup granulated sugar	1 T. vanilla
1/2 cup shortening	1/4 cup butter
1/4 cup (small can) evaporated milk	

Combine ingredients and beat 8–10 minutes. Spread between any cake you wish. Do not refrigerate.

Lisa Becker, Bethel Church of the Nazarene, Bethel, Ohio

CARAMEL SAUCE

1/4 cup butter	1 cup cold water
1 cup brown sugar	2 T. vanilla
1 T. cornstarch	

Melt butter in pan over medium heat. Add sugar, then cornstarch which has been dissolved in the water. Bring slowly to the boiling point, stirring to blend. Remove from heat; add vanilla.

Carolyn likes this served on squares of chocolate cake.

Carolyn Clubine, First United Methodist Church, Dunkerton, Iowa

Desserts

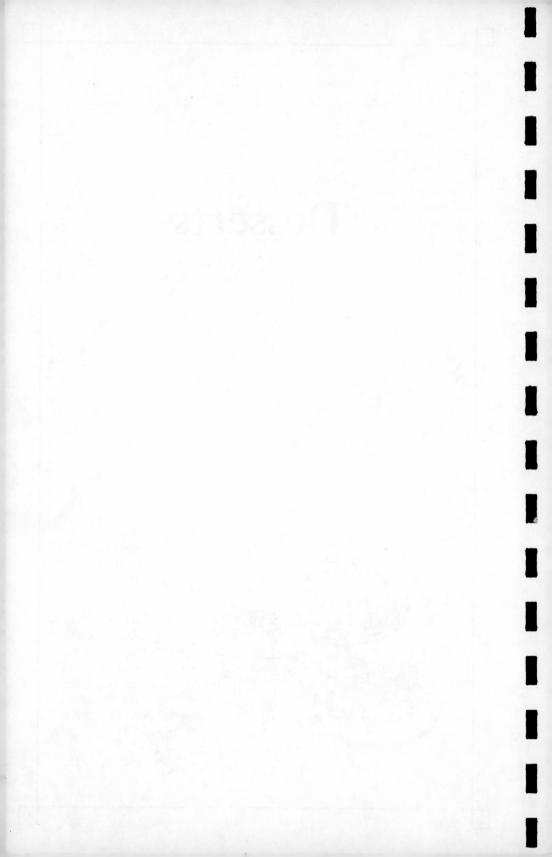

DESSERTS

RASPBERRY SQUARES

This is very popular at bake sales.

2 cups flour
3/4 cup shortening
Pinch of salt

1/2 cup *ice* water
8 oz. raspberry jam (or other jams of your choice)

In large bowl mix flour, shortening, and salt with pastry blender. Blend until dough has consistency of crumbs. Mix in *ice* water with fork and form into large ball. Split ball in half, being careful not to "play" with dough too much, as this makes it tough.

Roll out on floured cloth to shape of rectangular dimensions of a cookie sheet. Roll dough onto rolling pin and drop onto cookie sheet. Spread jam on top of dough evenly. Roll the other ball to the same dimension. Pick up with rolling pin and place on top of jam. Press edges together with fork. Spread with soft margarine on top of dough and brush with 1 tablespoon of milk. Bake at 425°F. for 15 minutes. Cut into squares—delicious!

Mrs. Peggy Farrar, South Main Street Congregational Church, Manchester, New Hampshire

RASPBERRY DESSERT

15 graham crackers,
  finely crushed
1/4 cup butter
1/2 lb. large marshmallows
1/2 cup milk

1 cup whipping cream
1-1/2 cups frozen raspberries
1 T. lemon or orange juice
1 t. flour or cornstarch

Mix cracker crumbs and butter. Put aside 1/4 cup crumbs. Put remainder on bottom of 8"x11" dish. Melt marshmallows in milk and cool. Whip cream and add to marshmallow mixture. Separate raspberries from juice and thicken juice with flour or cornstarch. Add lemon or orange juice to berries. Pour half marshmallow mixture over crumbs. Mix berries and juice, and pour over marshmallow mixture. Top with crumbs. Place in refrigerator for 4 hours (overnight). Serve with whipped cream and more raspberries.

Jean Bushell, Holy Cross Lutheran Church, Dodge City, Kansas

APPLE CRISP

1 cup oatmeal	10–12 apples, sliced
1 cup brown sugar	Sugar
1 cup flour	Cinnamon
1 cup margarine, melted	Nutmeg

Mix oatmeal, brown sugar, flour, and margarine. Pat half of the mixture into greased 8" pan. Add sliced apples and sprinkle with sugar, cinnamon, and nutmeg to taste. Place remaining oatmeal mixture on top. Bake at 350°F. for 40–60 minutes.

Can use recipe 1-1/2 times for a 9" pan.

Paula Sommerlot, Central Christian Church, Marshalltown, Iowa

BLUEBERRY/PEACH COBBLER

1/4 cup sugar	1 cup flour
1/4 cup brown sugar	1/2 cup sugar
1 T. cornstarch	1-1/2 t. baking powder
1/2 cup water	1/2 t. salt
1 t. lemon juice	1/2 cup milk
2 cups peaches, sliced	1/4 cup butter
(4 medium size peaches)	2 T. sugar
1 cup blueberries	1/4 t. nutmeg

Combine first 4 ingredients in saucepan. Cook on medium heat, stirring until thick. Add next 3 ingredients. Pour into 8" square pan. Sift flour, sugar, baking powder, and salt. Add milk and butter; spoon over fruit. Sprinkle with mixture of sugar and nutmeg. Bake at 375°F. for 30–35 minutes.

Patty Metz, Bethany United Methodist Church, Latrobe, Pennsylvania

BLUEBERRY BUCKLE

3/4 cup sugar	1/2 t. salt
1/4 cup butter, melted	1/2 cup milk
1 egg	2 cups blueberries
2 t. baking powder	2 cups flour

Combine sugar, butter, egg, and milk. Mix well. Blend in flour, baking powder, and salt; mix well. Stir in blueberries. Pour into buttered 9"x9" pan. Sprinkle topping over batter. Bake at 375°F. for 30–35 minutes.

TOPPING

1/2 cup sugar	1/4 cup butter
1 t. cinnamon	

Combine ingredients and mix until crumbly. Sprinkle over batter.

Marilyn Rainbolt, First Baptist Church, Jonesboro, Arkansas

GRANDMA'S APPLE DESSERT

2 cups sugar
1/2 cup shortening
2 eggs, beaten
2 cups flour
2 t. baking soda
1 t. cinnamon
1/2 t. nutmeg

1/2 t. salt
1/4 cup milk
4 cups apples, finely chopped
1/2 cup raisins
1/2 cup nuts, chopped
1 t. vanilla

Cream sugar and shortening; add eggs, mix well. Add sifted dry ingredients and milk. Add apples (pack apples in measured amount), raisins, nuts, and vanilla. Mix well. Bake in greased and floured 9"x13" pan at 325°F. for 1 hour or until done. Cut into serving pieces and garnish as described below.

SAUCE FOR TOP

1 cup sugar
2 T. flour
1 cup boiling water

1/2 cup butter
1 t. vanilla

Mix sugar and flour together; add boiling water slowly over mixture. Add butter and cook until thick. Add vanilla. Spread over warm baked cake.

Juanita serves this dessert garnished with sweetened whipping cream and maraschino cherries.

Juanita Kendall, Grantville United Methodist Church, North Topeka, Kansas

LUCY MAE'S CANDIED APPLES

A favorite at church dinners.

2 large Rome apples
3/4 cup sugar

1/2 cup water
Dash of salt

Be sure apples are the cooking variety. Leave apples unpeeled. Quarter and core each piece. Place in pan large enough so as not to crowd pieces. Cover with sugar and add water. Cover and bring to a boil; lower heat to simmering and cook until tender. If juice remains too thin, remove apples and add small amount of sugar and cook a little longer. Pour juice over apples (juice should jell as in apple jelly).

Very pretty served in a nice glass dish or bowl.

Nell Barbee, Fairview Cumberland Presbyterian Church, Marshall, Texas

INEZ'S APRICOT CRUNCH

2 cans apricot pie filling
1 regular pkg. cake mix, dry
   (white or yellow)

1 stick margarine, melted
Cool Whip or a whipped topping
Coconut (optional)

Pour 2 cans apricot pie filling into 7-1/2"x11-1/2" pyrex baking dish. Sprinkle cake mix over top of pie filling. Drizzle margarine over top. Bake at 350°F. until top is slightly brown. Cool, then serve with whipped topping. Sprinkle coconut over top, if desired.

Mrs. Susie Stout, Peru First Brethren Church, Peru, Indiana

RHUBARB DESSERT

4 cups rhubarb, cut up
1 cup sugar
1 pkg. white or yellow
   cake mix

1 pkg. cherry or strawberry
   gelatin
1 cup water
1 stick margarine

Put rhubarb in 9"x13" cake pan. Sprinkle sugar over rhubarb. Sprinkle box of gelatin over sugar. Sprinkle dry cake mix over gelatin. Sprinkle water over gelatin and cake mix. Melt margarine and drizzle evenly over top. Bake at 350°F. about 40 minutes. Watch after 30 minutes; it might not take the full 40 minutes. Let stand until cool. Cut in squares and serve with whipped topping or whipped cream. Good!

Mrs. Eleanor M. Tweito, Redeemer Lutheran Church, Marshall, Missouri

RHUBARB TORTE

1 cup flour
1 T. sugar
1/2 cup butter
3 egg yolks
3 cups rhubarb, cut
1 cup sugar

2 T. flour
3 egg whites
6 T. sugar
1/2 cup cream
Flaked coconut
Chopped nuts

Mix first 3 ingredients and put in 9"x9" pan. Bake at 350°F. for 10 minutes. Beat egg yolks; add sugar, cream, and flour. Stir in diced rhubarb and pour over baked crust. Return to oven for 40 minutes. Remove from oven and spread with egg whites that have been beaten stiff and sugar added. Sprinkle with coconut and nuts. Return to oven until browned slightly.

Martha Sundell, Zion Evangelical Lutheran Church, McHenry, Illinois

LEMON BISQUE

1—3 oz. pkg. lemon gelatin
1-1/2 cups boiling water
2–3 T. lemon juice
1/2 cup sugar

1 large can cold evaporated
 cream (must be refrigerated
 overnight)

Dissolve lemon gelatin with boiling water. Add lemon juice and sugar. Put into refrigerator until it jells. Beat evaporated cream (milk), that has been refrigerated night before, until peaks form. Fold into jelled mixture and pour into crust. Sprinkle saved crumbs on top and put into refrigerator.

This dessert should be made the day before it is to be served for the best results.

CRUST

1-1/3 cups graham crumbs
1/4 cup sugar

1/2 cup butter or margarine,
 melted

Mix and press ingredients onto bottom of 9''x13'' pan. Save some crumbs for topping.

Alberta Werkmeister, First Presbyterian Church, Belmar, New Jersey

GRANDMA'S CREAM PUFFS

FILLING

12 T. flour
1 cup sugar
1/2 t. salt
4 cups milk

4 eggs, beaten
2 T. margarine
2 t. vanilla

Make filling first, so it can cool. Thoroughly mix flour, half the sugar, and salt. Gradually add scalded milk, stirring constantly until thickened. Remove. Add eggs and remaining sugar. Cook 1 minute, remove and add margarine and vanilla. Cool.

PUFFS

1/2 cup margarine
1 cup boiling water
1 cup flour

1/2 t. salt
4 eggs, beaten

Melt margaine in boiling water, stir in flour and salt all at once. Stir well until mixture leaves sides of pan in a mass. Remove from heat. Quickly stir in beaten eggs until smooth. Drop on baking sheet. Bake at 450°F. for 10 minutes. Then 400°F. for 25 minutes. Cool. Cut top off and fill. Dust with powdered sugar or make chocolate glaze.

Pauline Robinson, Perryton Presbyterian Church, Aledo, Illinois

MILK CHOCOLATE MOUSSE

1—6 oz. pkg. semi-sweet
   chocolate pieces
1/3 cup water
1/2 cup sugar

1/8 t. salt
2 eggs, separated
1 t. vanilla
2 cups cream for whipping

Combine chocolate pieces and water in small saucepan; heat slowly, stirring constantly until chocolate melts and mixture is smooth. Stir in 1/4 cup sugar and salt; heat, stirring constantly until sugar dissolves. Remove from heat. Beat egg yolks slightly in small bowl. Very slowly beat in hot chocolate mixture and vanilla; cool.

Beat egg whites until foamy-white and double in volume in medium size bowl. Beat in remaining 1/4 cup sugar, 1 tablespoon at a time, until meringue stands in firm peaks. Beat cream until stiff in a second medium size bowl. Fold cooled chocolate mixture into meringue, then fold in whipping cream until no streaks of white remain. Pour into 8'' spring-form pan; cover. Freeze 6 hours or until firm. When ready to serve, loosen around edge with a knife, release spring and carefully lift off side of pan.

Darlene L. Espinoza, Sebastopol Christian Church, Sebastopol, California

ECLAIR DESSERT SQUARES

1 box whole graham crackers
2 pkgs. instant French Vanilla
   pudding

1—9 oz. container whipped
   topping
Chopped nuts

Butter bottom of 9''x13'' baking pan. Line with crackers, putting them close together. Mix pudding and add whipped topping. Pour half of mixture over crackers. Layer again, ending with crackers. Top with chocolate icing.

CHOCOLATE ICING

2 squares bitter chocolate,
   melted
2 t. white corn syrup
1 t. vanilla

1 T. butter
1-1/2 cups confectioners sugar
3 T. milk

Mix and spread on crackers. Sprinkle with nuts.

Prepare squares 2 days ahead. Serves 12.

Joyce Yount, Prince of Peace Lutheran Church, Hot Springs, Arkansas

CHOCOLATE REFRIGERATOR CAKE

6 oz. sweet chocolate,
cut in small pieces
1/4 cup water
4 eggs, separated
2 T. sugar

1 cup heavy cream, chilled
1 t. vanilla
3 dozen single ladyfingers
1/2 cup nutmeats, broken

Melt chocolate in water over hot water; cool. Beat egg yolks until thick and lemon colored. Add chocolate mixture and sugar; mix well. Chill. Fold in whipped cream, nuts, vanilla, and stiffly beaten egg whites. Line bottom and side of 9'' spring-form pan with ladyfingers, placing rounded side next to pan. Cover with half of filling; cover filling with remaining ladyfingers. Spread remaining filling on top. Chill in refrigerator about 8 hours.

Betty Hrnjak, West Allis Baptist Church, West Allis, Wisconsin

BETHEL BANANA SPLIT

3 sticks margarine
2 cups (12 oz. box) vanilla
wafers or graham crackers,
crushed
1 large container Cool Whip
1 large can crushed pineapple

2 eggs
2 cups powdered sugar
6 small or 3-1/2 large bananas
1 jar maraschino cherries
1 cup nuts, crushed/chopped

Melt 1 stick margarine and add to crushed vanilla wafers. Press mixture into large pan, 13''x9''x2''. Beat eggs, 2 sticks margarine, and powdered sugar with mixer for 15 minutes. Then spread mixture over crust in pan. Cover with sliced bananas and well drained pineapple. Spread Cool Whip on top. Dot with cherries and sprinkle with crushed nuts. Best if refrigerated overnight.

Nancy Becker, Bethel Church of the Nazarene, Bethel, Ohio

COCONUT/ALMOND DELIGHT

1 cup coconut
1/2 cup almonds, slivered
Grated rind of 1 orange
1 can Eagle Brand sweetened, condensed milk

1 —6 oz. can frozen orange
juice concentrate
1 cup sour cream

Toast the coconut and the almonds separately in oven; when cool, add the grated orange rind. Mix all other ingredients together. Layer in sherbet glasses, ending with coconut-almond mixture.

This is delicious!

Arlis J. Enburg, Memorial Heights United Methodist Church, Rock Island, Illinois

CARMALLOW APPLE SWIRL

2 cups oatmeal cookie crumbs
1/3 cup margarine, melted
1—12 oz. jar caramel topping
2—7 oz. jars marshmallow
  creme
1—8 oz. pkg. Philadelphia cream cheese, softened

2—8 oz. containers La Creme
  whipped topping with
  real cream
3/4 cup apple butter
1/4 cup walnuts, chopped

Combine crumbs and margarine; press onto bottom of 9'' spring-form pan. Reserve 1/4 cup caramel topping. Combine remaining caramel topping, marshmallow creme, and softened cream cheese. Mix at medium speed with electric mixer until well blended. Fold in 1 container whipped topping. Add apple butter; cut through mixture with knife several times for marble effect. Pour over crust; freeze. Top with remaining whipped topping and walnuts. Makes 12–14 servings.

Dolores King, Calvary Baptist Church, Judsonia, Arkansas

AGATHA'S CHEESE CAKE

1-1/4 cups graham cracker
  crumbs
1/4 cup butter, softened
1/4 cup sugar
1 cup (6 oz.) semi-sweet
  chocolate
1 cup sugar

24 oz. cream cheese, softened
1/4 cup flour
1 T. vanilla
6 eggs, separated
1 cup sour cream
Pinch of salt

Mix first 3 ingredients well, spread on bottom and sides of spring-form pan. Melt chocolate in top of double boiler. Cream sugar and cream cheese together in large bowl. Add salt and beat until creamy. Stir in flour and vanilla. Add egg yolks, one at a time, beating well after each. Stir in sour cream. Beat egg whites to soft peaks and fold into mixture. Remove 1-3/4 cups mixture to a smaller bowl and add melted chocolate to remaining mixture. Pour 1/2–3/4 of chocolate mixture into crust. Cover with plain mixture; then spoon rest of chocolate mixture over top. Marble with spatula.

Place cake in preheated 400°F. oven. Immediately reset oven to 300°F. Bake for 1 hour. Turn oven off, but allow cheesecake to remain in warm oven 45 minutes. Cool thoroughly. Chill overnight. Serves 10–12.

Susan Tillie, Valley Christian Center, San Dimas, California

CHEESE CAKE

GRAHAM CRACKER CRUST

1-1/4 cups graham cracker   1/4 cup sugar
    crumbs   1/4 cup butter, softened

Make crust of above ingredients. Pour crumb mixture into 9'' or 10''
spring-form pan and press crumb mixture firmly against bottom of
pan. Save 1/4 cup crumb mixture to sprinkle on top of sour cream
mixture at end.

FILLING

3—8 oz. pkgs. cream cheese   4 eggs
1 cup sugar   2 t. vanilla

Put cream cheese, at room temperature, into a bowl. Beat with sugar
and then add 4 eggs, one at a time, and beat well after addition of each
egg. Then add vanilla and beat well. Pour into graham cracker crust.
Bake in preheated oven at 325°F. for about 1 hour or until the center
is firm. Remove from oven for 10 minutes. Meantime, raise oven
temperature to 450°F. and mix the topping.

TOPPING

1 pt. sour cream   1-1/2 t. vanilla
1/2 cup sugar

Spread topping over cream cheese mixture, sprinkle crumb mixture on
topping and bake for 5 minutes only. Remove from oven and cool in
pan on a wire rack, away from drafts. Refrigerate several hours or
overnight before serving.

Rev. Paul W. Bowles, Ossining United Methodist Church, Ossining, New York

ICE CREAM DESSERT

1 small pkg. Oreo cookies
4 small Butterfinger candy bars

1 stick margarine, melted
1/2 gallon ice cream

Crush Oreo cookies and Butterfinger candy bars. Mix together with the melted margarine. Press in 12"x15" dish half of mixture. Put ice cream on top. Put other half of cookie mixture on top of ice cream. Freeze. Cut into squares to serve.

Emma Jean Snook, El Monte Wesleyan Church, El Monte, California

HOMEMADE PEANUT BUTTER ICE CREAM

2 cups granulated sugar
1—13 oz. can evaporated milk
1—14 oz. can sweetened
  condensed milk
1 t. vanilla

3 eggs
Dash salt
1 cup crunchy peanut butter
Milk

Mix together sugar, evaporated milk, sweetened condensed milk, vanilla, eggs, salt, and peanut butter. Put into hand or electric ice cream freezer canister and add enough milk to bring mixture up to the 2/3 line. Freeze until firm. Makes about 4 quarts.

Lois DeHart, Woodlawn Baptist Church, Conover, North Carolina

HOMEMADE MINT CHOCOLATE CHIP ICE CREAM

1 qt. half-and-half
1 qt. extra rich milk
1 pt. whipping cream
1—1-1/2 lbs. sugar
  (or sweeten to taste)

1 t. vanilla
Pure mint extract to taste
Green food coloring
1—12 oz. pkg. Nestle's tiny
  morsels

Mix together half-and-half, milk, and whipping cream. Add sugar to taste. Add vanilla, mint extract, and food coloring. Pour into container, then add full package of Nestle's tiny morsels and start cranking. Let it set up about 20–25 minutes then check—enjoy!

Rev. Gary Winkleman, Thurston Christian Church, Springfield, Oregan

DE-LITE FRUIT BOWL

2 large red delicious apples,
    cut in thin wedges
    (leave skin on for color)
1 large green Granny Smith
    apple, cut in thick wedges
    (leave skin on for color)
4 bananas, peeled and
    thickly sliced
2–4 oranges, peeled, seeded,
    and chunked

1—#2 can pineapple chunks,
    natural juice drained off
1 cup green seedless grapes
Sliced peaches, drained if using
    canned (optional)
Sliced pears, drained if using
    canned (optional)
1/2 cup orange juice
1 cup coconut, shredded
Blueberries or strawberries

Use a large brandy snifter, glass bowl or individual serving dishes. Place fruit in layers, alternating different colors and ending with bananas. Pour orange juice over fruit, making sure bananas are covered to keep from discoloring. You may use more juice if you prefer. Sprinkle on coconut and garnish with blueberries or strawberries.

Easy to prepare, light in calories and great with assorted cheeses for luncheons or dessert course.

Reta B. Kirsh, First United Methodist Church, Mansfield, Ohio

WATERMELON AMBROSIA

1/2 watermelon, cut out,
    leaving 1'' red
1 medium jar maraschino
    cherries
1—#303 can fruit cocktail
1 can mandarin oranges

1 large can pineapple cubes
1 cup mini colored
    marshmallows
1 medium pkg. coconut
1 cup 7-Up
4 medium bananas

Cut center of watermelon into bite-size pieces; add drained fruit. Mix fruit and marshmallows in watermelon cavity; pour part of 7-Up over mixture. Sprinkle with coconut. Refrigerate. When ready to serve, slice bananas and pour remaining 7-Up over fruit mixture.

Marybeth Leonard, Glad Tidings Assembly of God, Clearfield, Pennsylvania

FROZEN STRAWBERRY DESSERT

3/4 cup sugar
2 T. lemon juice
1—10 oz. pkg. frozen
strawberries

3 egg whites
1—8 oz. container Cool Whip
1 pkg. Pecan Sandies

Crush cookies and pat 2/3 into 9''x13'' pan. Reserve balance for topping. Beat sugar, lemon juice, egg whites and thawed strawberries for 8 minutes, fold in Cool Whip and spread over crumbs in pan. Top with reserved crumbs. Freeze. Do not defrost to serve.

Rose Schock, Palma Sola Presbyterian Church, Bradenton, Florida

CURRIED FRUIT

1—1 lb. can peach halves
1 can apricot halves
1/4 cup butter
1/4—1/3 cup brown sugar
3—5 pieces cloves

1 can pineapple chunks
1 can pear halves
2—3 T. curry powder
1/2—3/4 cup fruit syrup

Drain all fruits and put into a casserole, reserving needed amount of syrup. Melt butter in skillet; add sugar and curry powder. Mix in syrup and heat for 3—5 minutes. Add mixture to fruit. Bake covered at 325°F. for 45 minutes.

Sarah MacQuarrie, Trinity Baptist Church, Lynnfield, Massachusetts

Cookies
and
Confections

COOKIES

CREAM WAFERS

These are great for showers.

1 cup soft butter	Granulated sugar
1/3 cup whipping cream	Creamy filling (see below)
2 cups flour	

Mix thoroughly butter, cream, and flour. Cover and chill. Heat oven to 375°F. Roll about one-third of dough at a time 1/8'' thick on floured cloth-covered board. Keep remaining dough chilled. Cut into 1-1/2'' rounds. Transfer rounds with spatula to piece of waxed paper that is heavily covered with granulated sugar. Place on ungreased baking sheet. Prick rounds with fork about 4 times. Bake 7–9 minutes or just until set, but not brown. Cool. Put cookies together in pairs with Creamy Filling.

CREAMY FILLING

1/4 cup soft butter or margarine	1 t. vanilla
3/4 cup confectioners sugar	Food coloring

Cream butter, sugar, and vanilla until smooth and fluffy. Tint with few drops of food coloring. Add few drops water, if necessary, for proper consistency.

Diana Wisely, Towerview Baptist Church, Belleville, Illinois

BUTTERMILK COOKIES WITH FROSTING

1 cup shortening	1 cup buttermilk
2 cups sugar	2 t. baking soda
2 eggs	2 t. baking powder
1/2 t. salt	1-1/2 t. vanilla
5 cups flour	

Cream together shortening, sugar, and eggs. Add buttermilk and vanilla and mix together well. Combine salt, flour, baking soda, and baking powder and mix into creamed mixture. Drop by teaspoonful onto ungreased cookie sheet. Flatten with drinking glass covered with a damp piece of cheesecloth. Bake at 350°F. for 10 minutes.

FROSTING

1/4 lb. butter or margarine	1/4 cup milk
1 lb. box powdered sugar	(can use buttermilk)
1/4 t. salt	1 t. vanilla

Blend ingredients together.

Judy Evans, Comstock United Methodist Church, Comstock, Michigan

NELLIE HARDENDORF'S SOFT SUGAR COOKIES

Made for the "crew" who helps prepare the newsletter for mailing.

1 cup sugar	3-1/2 cups sifted flour
1 cup brown sugar	2 t. baking powder
1/3 cup butter or margarine	1 t. cream of tartar
1/2 cup shortening	3/4 t. salt
2 eggs	3/4 t. baking soda
1 t. vanilla	1 t. nutmeg
1/2 t. lemon extract	1 cup buttermilk

Beat first 4 ingredients. Beat in next 3 ingredients. Sift dry ingredients and add alternately with buttermilk. Drop 2-1/2'' apart on greased pan. Spread with back of spoon. Have outer edges thicker than center. Sprinkle with sugar. Bake at 400°F. for 10 minutes.

For softer cookies, bake at 410°F. for 8 minutes or when indentation remains when testing center.

Maxine Pihlaja, American Lutheran Church, Billings, Montana

ILA'S BEST SUGAR COOKIES

1 cup granulated sugar	1 t. vanilla
1 cup powdered sugar	1 t. cream of tartar
1 cup margarine	1 t. baking soda
1 cup oil	4 cups plus 4 T. flour
2 eggs	

Cream sugars, oil, and margarine. Add eggs and vanilla. Sift together dry ingredients and add to wet ingredients. Roll into small balls, place on cookie sheet and press with bottom of a drinking glass dipped in sugar. Bake at 350°F. for 8–10 minutes. Makes 6 dozen or more.

Gabi Stepp, Sunrise Bible Church, North Branch, Minnesota

BROWN SUGAR BROWNIES

1-1/3 cups sifted all-purpose flour	1 cup light brown sugar, packed
1 t. baking powder	1 egg
1/2 t. salt	1 t. vanilla
1/2 cup softened butter	1/2 cup pecans, chopped
	1—6 oz. pkg. chocolate morsels

Sift flour, salt, and baking powder; set aside. Cream butter and sugar. Add egg and stir well. Add this to flour mixture. Add vanilla, chocolate morsels, and pecans; stir well. Spread in a baking pan and bake at 350°F. for 20–25 minutes. Cool, then cut into bars.

Deborah P. Massey, First Presbyterian Church, Covington, Georgia

FAVORITE BROWNIES

1 cup shortening or
    2 sticks margarine
4 oz. unsweetened chocolate
4 eggs
2 cups sugar

2 t. vanilla
2 cups nuts, chopped
1-1/2 cups flour
1 t. salt
1 t. baking powder

Melt chocolate and margarine in saucepan; cool. Sift dry ingredients together. Add sugar and eggs to cooled mixture and mix well. Add dry ingredients, nuts, and vanilla. Pour in 13''x9'' greased pan. Bake at 350°F. for 25–30 minutes.

Agnes Dunning, First United Methodist Church, Titusville, Pennsylvania

CARAMEL NUT BROWNIES

50 caramels (14 oz. pkg.)
2/3 cup evaporated milk
1 pkg. German chocolate
    cake mix

3/4 cup butter or margarine,
    melted
1 cup chocolate chips
1 cup pecans, chopped

Melt caramels with 1/3 cup milk in top of double boiler over barely simmering water. Stir frequently. Combine cake mix with melted butter and remaining 1/3 cup milk. Spread half of this mixture into a greased 9''x13'' pan. Bake at 350°F. for 6–8 minutes. Remove from oven and sprinkle with chocolate chips and pecans. Drizzle melted caramels over chips and nuts. Cover with remaining cake batter. Continue baking at 350°F. for 15 minutes or until brownies are firm to the touch. Cool before slicing. Makes 3–4 dozen.

If second half of batter gets too dry, add a little more milk to spreading consistency.

June Roberts, First Baptist Church, Los Alamos, New Mexico

CHOCOLATE-CARAMEL BARS

1 cup brown sugar
1 cup butter
2 T. cream

Graham crackers
4 Hershey bars

Line jelly roll pan with foil. Grease foil and put layer of graham crackers on foil. Boil sugar, butter, and cream 1 minute and 40 seconds. Pour on graham crackers. Place in a 400°F. oven until it bubbles (about 3–5 minutes). Remove from oven and lay Hershey bars on top. Let melt and spread. Add chopped nuts if desired.

Joyce Tabor, Fairview Evangelical Church, Minnetonka, Minnesota

NUT GOODIE BARS

1/4 cup vanilla pudding mix
   (*not* instant)
1/2 cup evaporated milk
1 cup butter or margarine
2 lbs. powdered sugar
1 t. vanilla

2 cups creamy peanut butter
1 lb. *salted* peanuts
1—12 oz. pkg. chocolate chips
1—12 oz. pkg. butterscotch
   chips

Melt all chips and peanut butter. Spread half of this mixture on a 10''x15'' pan. Freeze until ready to fill. Bring pudding, milk, and butter to a boil. Take off burner. Add vanilla and powdered sugar, stirring until smooth. Spread on frozen layer. Add peanuts to remaining half of chocolate mixture. Spread on top of pudding layer. Return to freezer. Cut into bars *when firm!*

Serve right from freezer or keep in refrigerator. Absolutely delicious!

Marlene Tangen, Gethsemane Lutheran Church, St. Paul, Minnesota

CONGO SQUARES

1-1/2 sticks margarine
1 lb. light brown sugar
3 eggs
2-3/4 cups plain flour

1 t. baking powder
1/4 t. salt
1—6 oz. pkg. chocolate chips
1 cup nuts, chopped

Melt margarine and pour over brown sugar. Add eggs, flour, baking powder, and salt. Mix well. Fold in chocolate chips and nuts. Bake at 350°F. for 40–45 minutes in a 9''x13'' baking dish or pan. Cut while still warm. Easy to make and very good!

Nancy F. Pilant, Alice Bell Baptist Church, Knoxville, Tennessee

O'HENRY BARS

1 cup butter
1/2 cup sugar

1 cup brown sugar
4 cups oatmeal, uncooked

Cream butter. Add sugars and cream. Add oatmeal and mix well. Press into a well-greased 10''x15'' pan. Bake at 350°F. for only 12 minutes. Spread frosting over oatmeal mixture. Cool.

FROSTING

1 cup milk chocolate chips

1 cup peanut butter

Melt chocolate chips; mix with peanut butter. Spread over bars.

Claudia Ranslem, Arlington Community Church, Arlington, Nebraska

ROCKY ROAD COOKIES

1—6 oz. pkg. chocolate chips
1/2 cup butter or margarine
2 eggs
1 cup sugar
1-1/2 cups flour
1/2 t. baking powder

1/4 t. salt
1/2 t. vanilla
1 cup nuts, chopped
About 4 dozen miniature
    marshmallows, if desired

Melt 1/2 cup chocolate bits and butter over low heat; cool. Heat oven to 400°F. Mix remaining chocolate bits, eggs, sugar, flour, baking powder, salt, vanilla, nuts, and chocolate mixture. Drop dough by rounded teaspoonfuls 2'' apart onto an ungreased baking sheet. Press a marshmallow into center of each. Bake 8 minutes or until almost no imprint remains when touched with finger. Immediately remove from baking sheet. Makes about 4 dozen cookies.

Audrey Warren, Court Street United Methodist Church, Flint, Michigan

PEANUT BUTTER CHOCOLATE CHIP COOKIES

This is Renie's own original recipe.

1/2 cup butter or margarine
1/2 cup peanut butter
1/2 cup sugar
1/2 cup brown sugar
1 egg
1 t. vanilla

1 cup flour
1/4 t. salt
3/4 t. baking soda
2 T. water
1—6 oz. pkg. chocolate chips

Cream together butter, peanut butter, and sugars. Add egg, vanilla, and water. Beat well. Add dry ingredients and mix well. Stir in chocolate chips. Drop onto greased cookie sheets and bake in preheated 375°F. oven for 10–12 minutes or until nicely browned. Makes 3 dozen cookies.

Renie Larson, Kirk of Our Savior Presbyterian Church, Westland, Michigan

ساير

ggmlಿದ

PEANUT BUTTER/CINNAMON COOKIES

1/2 cup butter or margarine, softened
1/2 cup creamy peanut butter
1/2 cup sugar
1/2 cup brown sugar, firmly packed
1 egg
1 t. vanilla extract
1-1/4 cups all-purpose flour
1/2 t. baking soda
1/2 t. salt
1 t. ground cinnamon

Cream butter and peanut butter; gradually add sugar, beating until light and fluffy. Add egg and vanilla, beating well. Combine flour, baking soda, salt, and cinnamon; add to creamed mixture, mixing well. Shape dough into 36—1" balls; place 2" apart on lightly greased cookie sheets. Dip a fork in water and flatten cookies to 1/4" thickness. Bake at 350°F. for 12–14 minutes. Let cool 2 minutes on cookie sheets. Remove to wire racks and let cool completely. Makes 3 dozen cookies.

Edith M. Tussing, Allendale United Methodist Church, St. Petersburg, Florida

PEANUT BUTTER SANDWICH COOKIES

1 pkg. Ritz crackers or 1 pkg. club crackers
Peanut butter
1—12 oz. pkg. white almond bark
1—12 oz. pkg. semi-sweet chocolate morsels

Spread peanut butter between 2 crackers, making sandwiches. Melt almond bark and chocolate pieces together in a large bowl in microwave or in top of double boiler. Completely coat sandwiches by dipping in melted chocolate mixture. Set cookies on waxed paper to completely cool.

Deloris Heminger, First United Methodist Church, Wood River, Nebraska

OATMEAL COOKIES DELUXE

1 cup shortening
1 cup brown sugar
1 cup white sugar
2 eggs
1 t. baking soda
1 t. vanilla
1-1/2 cups flour
1 t. salt
1 t. cinnamon
3 cups quick oats
1/2 cup raisins, nuts, *or* chocolate chips

Cream shortening and sugars. Add the eggs, well beaten. Add vanilla. Add flour, salt, baking soda, and cinnamon. Add oats and raisins, nuts *or* chocolate chips. Bake at 350°F. for 10 minutes.

Beatrice Bullard, St. Andrew's Episcopal Church, Burt, New York

MONSTER COOKIES

Plan to spend awhile baking these, but they are well worth the effort. These are great crowd-pleasers with youth groups, traveling choral groups, etc. But "big people" like them, too. Terrific bake sale item!

1 dozen eggs
2 lbs. brown sugar
4 cups granulated sugar
1 T. vanilla
1 T. white Karo syrup
8 t. baking soda
1 lb. butter or margarine
3 lbs. extra crunchy peanut butter

18 cups quick type oatmeal
(1 large drum plus 2 cups)
1 lb. chocolate chips
1 lb. plain M&M's
(Yes, you are reading this right—quantities are very large!)

Mix in order of listed ingredients. Drop by ice cream scoop onto ungreased cookie sheets and flatten. Bake in a 375°F. oven for 12 minutes. Insert toothpick to see if they are done. Makes 10-1/2 dozen large cookies.

You may want to divide ingredients in half, mixing one half at a time, as this dough becomes very stiff and you will probably get it mixed better than doing an entire batch at once. You may just want to do half a batch if you don't want so many cookies at once, although they freeze beautifully.

Cyndi Steele, First Christian Church, Kennewick, Washington

MOLASSES CRINKLES

3/4 cup soft shortening
1 cup brown sugar, packed
1 egg
1/4 cup molasses
2-1/4 cups flour

2 t. baking soda
1/4 t. salt
1 t. cinnamon
1 t. ginger

Mix thoroughly shortening, sugar, egg, and molasses. Stir in remaining ingredients. Chill dough. Heat oven to 375°F. Roll dough into balls the size of large walnuts. Dip tops in sugar. Place sugar-side up 3'' apart on greased baking sheets. Sprinkle each cookie with 2–3 drops of water for a crackled surface. Bake 9–10 minutes or just until set, but not hard. Makes 4 dozen cookies.

Ms. Lorraine Misner, Townsend Congregational Church, Townsend, Massachusetts

SHORTBREAD

2 sticks butter
1 cup powdered sugar, sifted

3-1/2 cups all-purpose flour
  sifted

Mix all ingredients in large bowl with hands. Press into 8'' square pan. Bake at 325 °F. for 55–60 minutes until golden brown. Cut into squares immediately. Remove from pan immediately. Cool on wire rack. Store in air-tight can.

Mrs. Amy Myers, Eastminster Presbyterian Church, Knoxville, Tennessee

SWEDISH COOKIES

1/2 lb. (1 cup) butter
1/2 cup powdered sugar
1-3/4 cups cake flour

1 cup walnuts, chopped
1 t. vanilla

Cream butter and add sugar slowly. Add flour; add nuts; add flavoring. Chill in refrigerator 1 hour or longer. Roll in small balls by hand. Bake at 350 °F. for 20 minutes. Roll in powdered sugar; coat twice. Pack in air-tight jar. Makes approximately 36–48 balls. These are excellent.

Mrs. Ruth Carothers, Our Saviour's Lutheran Church, Whispering Pines, North Carolina

ING'S SQUARES

1/4 cup butter
2 cups brown sugar
2 eggs, separated
1 cup nutmeats

1-1/2 cups flour
2 t. baking powder
1 t. vanilla

Cream butter together with 1 cup brown sugar; add egg yolks. Sift flour together with baking powder; add to mixture. Stir well and add 1/2 teaspoon vanilla. Pat mixture into a 9''x9'' cake pan; sprinkle nutmeats over this. Beat egg whites very stiff and beat in second cup of brown sugar and 1/2 teaspoon vanilla; spread over the top of the nuts. Bake in a 350 °F. oven for 30 minutes. Cut into squares and serve.

Mrs. Fred Prehm, Cowlitz Prairie Baptist Church, Winlock, Washington

LEMON BARS

1 cup (2 sticks) butter or margarine	4 eggs
1/4 t. salt	4 T. lemon juice
1/2 cup powdered sugar	2 cups sugar
2 cups flour	4 T. flour
	Grated rind of 1 lemon

Blend first 4 ingredients and press into a greased 10"x13" baking dish. Bake at 350°F. for 18–20 minutes or until browned. Mix remaining ingredients and pour over first mixture; bake at 325°F. for approximately 20 minutes or until firm. Dust with powdered sugar and cut when cool. Keep in refrigerator.

Ruth Crocker, Riverside Baptist Church, San Antonio, Texas

MERRY CHERRY CHEESECAKE BARS

Nice for Christmas.

CRUST

1/3 cup butter or margarine   1 cup all-purpose flour
1/3 cup brown sugar, firmly packed

Preheat oven 350°F. In 1-quart mixer bowl, cut butter in chunks; add brown sugar and flour; mix at low speed. Beat at medium speed, scraping sides of bowl often, until well mixed (1 minute). Reserve 1/2 cup crumb mixture for topping. Press remaining crumb mixture into 8" square baking pan. Bake near center of 350°F. oven for 10–12 minutes. Prepare filling. Spread filling over crust; sprinkle with remaining crumb mixture. Continue baking for 18–20 minutes or until filling is set and top is lightly browned. Cool. Store in refrigerator.

FILLING

8 oz. cream cheese, softened	1/4 cup glazed red cherries, chopped
1/4 cup sugar	
1 egg	1/4 cup glazed green cherries, chopped
1 T. lemon juice	

In 1-quart mixer bowl, beat cream cheese, sugar, egg, and lemon juice at medium speed until fluffy (1–2 minutes). Stir in chopped cherries.

Janet Mann, St. John Lutheran Church, Romeo, Michigan

CHERRY TARTS

You will need small tart pans.

FILLING

1 t. vanilla	2 cups sugar
1 egg	6 oz. cream cheese, softened

Combine all together. Mix until just blended (do not beat); set aside.

CRUSTS

2 cups flour	6 oz. cream cheese, softened
2 sticks margarine	

Mix all ingredients with hands until well blended and not sticky. Form into a ball and set in freezer for 5 minutes. Remove from freezer; form into 48 small balls, flatten, and place into small tart pans loosely. Fill three-fourths full with filling; bake at 350°F. for 20 minutes until light brown. Remove from pans; cool. Place small dab of sour cream in each, then a small dab of cherry preserves on top.

Mrs. John F. Amstutz, Ferris Church of Christ, Vestaburg, Michigan

ANISE TOAST (ITALIAN COOKIE)

1/2 cup margarine	1/4 t. almond flavoring
1 cup sugar	1 t. vanilla flavoring
1/4 t. salt	1 t. lemon flavoring
5 eggs	2 t. anise
2-1/2 cups flour	1/2 cup walnuts, chopped
3 t. baking powder	1/2 cup raisins (optional)

Preheat oven to 375°F. Cream together margarine, sugar, and salt. Then add eggs, 2 at a time; beat well. Add half the flour. Remove from mixer and add remaining flour, baking powder, and flavorings. Add nuts and/or raisins. Mix all ingredients well with wooden spoon. Grease and flour 2 cookie sheets. Spoon mixture onto 1 cookie sheet *only* to make 2 rows lengthwise. Pile high with spoons. Bake for 20 minutes. Remove from oven and cool for 4 minutes. Cut into 1'' slices and put back onto 2 cookie sheets. Turn oven to 425°F. and finish baking for 8 minutes.

Mary Ann Pepe, Covenant United Presbyterian Church, Sharon, Pennsylvania

CONFECTIONS

AMISH CARAMEL CORN

7 qts. popped corn
2 cups brown sugar
1/2 cup white Karo syrup
1 t. vanilla

1 t. salt
2 sticks margarine
1/2 t. baking soda
Pecans (optional)

Boil sugar, Karo syrup, margarine, and salt for 5 minutes. Remove from heat. Add baking soda and vanilla. Pour half the caramel mixture over half the popped corn and mix well. Add remaining popped corn and caramel and mix again. A large Dutch oven is perfect to do this in. Bake at 250 °F. for 1 hour. Remove from pan and put on paper to cool.

Sally Houston, Church of the Cross-United Methodist, Lexington, Ohio

QUICK AND EASY CARAMEL CORN FOR MICROWAVES

1 cup brown sugar, light or
   dark
1 stick margarine

4 cups Karo syrup, light or dark
2 t. salt

Combine all ingredients and boil 2 minutes. Remove from heat and stir in 1–2 teaspoons baking soda. Spray a large brown paper shopping bag with Pam or other non-stick spray. Pour 4 quarts of popped corn into sprayed bag and then pour in cooked caramel mixture. Microwave on High for 1-1/2 minutes then shake well. Microwave on High for 1 minute then shake well. Microwave on High for 1/2 minute. Eat and enjoy.

Reta B. Kirsh, First United Methodist Church, Mansfield, Ohio

SPICED PECANS

1 egg white
1/4 cup sugar

1 t. cinnamon
2 cups pecans

Beat egg white until frothy. Mix with sugar, cinnamon, and pecans. Spread on cookie sheet covered with foil. Cook in a 275 °F. oven for 30 minutes. Stir every 10 minutes to keep from sticking.

Lou Ann McGuire, First Baptist Church, Crescent, Oklahoma

PEPPERMINT ICE CANDY

3 individual chunks almond bark   3–4 drops red food coloring
4 crushed peppermint candies (individual pieces like Brach's)

Melt almond bark in microwave for 1 minute on High; stir; then 1 more minute on High. Add an additional 10 seconds, if necessary. Add remaining ingredients to melted bark. Stir well. Smooth out very thin on waxed paper. Break up or cut into bite-sized pieces when cooled. Store in an air-tight container.

Tastes just like Fanny May's peppermint ice candy!

Pat Stuckey, First Christian Church, Brazil, Indiana

PEANUT BRITTLE

2 cups sugar
1/2 cup white corn syrup
1/2 cup water
4 T. butter or margarine

2 cups raw Spanish peanuts
1 t. salt
1/2 t. vanilla
1/2 t. baking soda

Bring sugar, water, syrup, and butter to 260°F. on candy thermometer. Do not stir except to blend. Add raw peanuts, stirring constantly to 310°F. Add vanilla, salt, and baking soda. Pour onto 3 well-buttered cookie sheets. When cool enough to touch with well-buttered fingers, pull as thin as possible (The edges will begin to get firm. You will have to pull the outside edges, going from pan to pan).

This is super peanut brittle.

Nancy Handley, Nemaha Christian Church (Disciples of Christ), Nemaha, Nebraska

PEANUT PATTIES

2-1/2 cups sugar
2/3 cup white corn syrup
1 cup milk
1 t. butter or margarine

1 t. vanilla
3 or more drops red
    food coloring
3–4 cups raw peanuts

Mix sugar, peanuts, and milk in a large heavy pan (iron skillet is good). Cook for 1 hour at low temperature, starting on high heat and turning down when it starts to boil. Cook to soft ball on candy thermometer. It takes a long time, but no need to stand over it; just stir once in a while. Candy will have a brownish look when done and will taste done, also.

When cooked, set off heat and add butter, vanilla, and food coloring. Drop in greased muffin tins to make nice round patties or drop on cookie sheet in small mounds. Let set and store in covered dish or can, or wrap individually like candy bars with plastic wrap.

Glenda Findley, Westport Baptist Church, Cleveland, Oklahoma

FAVORITE CHOCOLATE-PEANUT BUTTER BALLS

1/2 cup margarine, melted
2 cups chunky peanut butter
1 lb. powdered sugar
4 cups Rice Krispies, rolled fine

1 giant Hershey bar
12 oz. chocolate chips
1/4 block paraffin

Combine margarine, peanut butter, and powdered sugar. Then add the minced Rice Krispies. Roll into walnut-sized balls. Place Hershey bar, chocolate chips, and paraffin in double boiler to melt. When chocolate mixture is thoroughly melted, dip balls into the mixture with fork. Completely cover the ball with chocolate mixture. Remove and place on waxed paper to cool. Keep refrigerated or in a cool place for storage. Makes 50–75 balls.

Kimberley Skaines, First Evangelical Free Church, Austin, Texas

CHOCOLATE-PEANUT BUTTER FUDGE

2 sticks margarine
1 box powdered sugar

1 cup peanut butter
8 oz. chocolate chips

Melt margarine; add powdered sugar and peanut butter. Pour into greased 11"x9" pan. Melt chocolate chips in double boiler and pour over fudge. After 15 minutes on counter, mark fudge and refrigerate. Cut in squares after 3–4 hours.

Mrs. Peggy Farrar, South Main Street Congregational Church, Manchester, New Hampshire

ALMOND TOFFEE

1 cup sugar
1 pkg. almond slivers
   (approximately 3 oz.)

2 sticks butter
3 T. water

Place all ingredients in heavy frying pan. Cook on high heat until light brown. Pour on cookie sheet, and spread thin; let cool. Break into pieces.

Lois Ann White, Stapley & Dana Church of Christ, Mesa, Arizona

MILLIONAIRES

1—12 oz. pkg. chocolate chips
2 T. water

1—14 oz. pkg. caramels
Pecan hunks

Melt caramels with water in a double boiler. Add chocolate chips and maybe a little more water. Mix well; add pecans. Stir and drop onto foil; let set.

Agnes Kasper, Zion Lutheran Church, Walburg, Texas

FUDGE

2 cups sugar
1 small can (2/3 cup)
  evaporated milk
12 regular size marshmallows
1/2 cup margarine

Few grains salt
1—6 oz. pkg. chocolate chips
1 cup pecans
1 t. vanilla

Mix sugar, milk, marshmallows, margarine, and salt in a heavy 2-quart saucepan. Cook, stirring constantly over medium heat. Boil. Mixture will be bubbling all over top. Boil 5 minutes more. Take off heat. Add chocolate chips; stir until chips are completely dissolved. Add pecans and vanilla. Pour in a greased 8'' pan; cool. Makes 30 pieces.

Willeen Bundick, Riverside Baptist Church, San Antonio, Texas

EASTER EGGS

3/4 lb. soft margarine
7 oz. marshmallow creme
12 oz. peanut butter, smooth type

1-1/2 lb. powdered sugar

Cream margarine and 1/2 pound sugar until fluffy. Add marshmallow, peanut butter, and 1 pound sugar. Cool; shape into eggs. Freeze 1 hour before dipping in a chocolate coating.

Mrs. Mitzi Caldwell, St. Andrew's United Methodist Church, Richmond, Virginia

Recipes
To Feed
A Crowd

RECIPES TO FEED A CROWD

CREAM OF TOMATO SOUP
Serves 200.

20—50 oz. cans condensed
   tomato soup
6 bunches celery, chopped fine
6 lbs. onions, chopped fine
8 cups brown sugar

4 cups butter
3/4–1 cup salt (to taste)
7 cups flour
4 gals. milk

Boil celery and onions in separate pans until tender. Put through food processor or blender. Blend flour, butter, and salt. Add brown sugar. Mix with celery; add onions. Slowly add tomato soup. Heat and slowly add milk. Bring to serving temperature. *Do not boil!*

Can be frozen; do not add milk until thawed and ready to serve.

Wilma Tracy, Our Savior's Lutheran Church, Rockford, Illinois

CINNAMON ROLLS
Makes about 50.

2 qts. water
2/3 cup yeast
2 cups sugar
6-1/2 lbs. flour (about 26 cups)*

1-1/2 cups dry milk
3 T. salt
1-1/2 cups oil or shortening
Cinnamon

Add warm water to yeast, shortening, and sugar. Add salt, milk, and enough flour to beat well (not quite half the flour). Add rest of flour gradually until dough pulls away from side of bowl. Take pieces of dough and knead until smooth. Roll out on floured surface to large rectangle. Brush with melted butter. Sprinkle with sugar and cinnamon to taste. Roll up and cut into 1'' wide pieces. Set aside covered and let rise until double. Bake at 350°F. for 20–25 minutes or until light brown. Frost with powdered sugar icing.

*Use 8 cups whole wheat flour and the rest unbleached white flour, if desired.

Karen Wagner, St. Timothy Lutheran Church, Portland, Oregon

AUNTIE LUCILLE PUNCH

Serves 100–125.

3—#3 cans pineapple juice
3 dozen lemons
6 lbs. sugar
12 sprigs of mint

8 qts. ginger ale
3 qts. water
Food coloring

Boil mint, sugar, lemon juice and lemon hulls in the 3 quarts water. Strain. Add fruit juice and food coloring (your choice, but green or pink is best). Store in the refrigerator. To serve, add 2 parts of the above mixture to 1 part ginger ale and 1 part water.

It will last for months in the refrigerator, so it's great for teas, parties, and especially for large church functions.

Deborah P. Massey, First Presbyterian Church, Covington, Georgia

BANQUET FRUIT CUP

Serves 120.

3—1 lb. 13 oz. cans pear halves
3—1 lb. 13 oz. cans sliced
    peaches
4—1 lb. cans pineapple chunks
5—1 lb. cans grapefruit sections
8—1 lb. cans chunky mixed fruit

5 small cans mandarin oranges
3 bottles maraschino cherries
3 qts. fresh strawberries
8-1/2 lbs. fresh bananas
3 qts. rainbow sherbet

Mix fruit in very large commercial pan or punch bowl. Fill plastic "old-fashioned" style glasses 1/2 full. Top with a miniature scoop of sherbet.

Approximately 35ᶜ per serving, but ingredients could be donated.

Mrs. Richard I. Gourley, First Congregational Church, Hopkinton, New Hampshire

CHEESE STRATA

Serves 90–100.

84 bread slices, trimmed
5-1/4 lbs. sharp cheese, sliced
7—10 oz. pkgs. frozen broccoli
14 cups ham, cubed
42 eggs

6 qts. plus 2-1/2 cups milk
14 t. dehydrated onion
3-1/2 t. salt
1-3/4 t. dry mustard

This amount fits into three 22-1/2"x12-1/2" steam-table-size pans. Grease pans. Layer bread slices, cheese, broccoli, and ham. Extra bread slices may be cut into triangles and put on top. Combine all other ingredients and pour over layered ingredients. This should be prepared a day ahead of time and allowed to stand in refrigerator overnight. Bake at 350°F. for 1 hour.

Mrs. Dee McCoy, Tabernacle Presbyterian Church, Indianapolis, Indiana

SHOO-FLY PIE

CRUMB MIXTURE

18 cups unsifted flour   1-1/2 lbs. margarine (6 sticks)
6 cups light brown sugar, packed

In large basin mix ingredients together with your hands until crumbly; reserve. Prepare wet mixture.

WET MIXTURE

8-1/2 cups baking molasses   6 t. baking soda
8-1/2 cups boiling water

Pour molasses and half of hot water into a large pan. In remaining hot water, mix baking soda and stir until foamy. Add to molasses and water mixture. Stir until foamy again. Pour a generous 1-1/2 cups molasses mixture into 10 pastry lined pans. Carefully sprinkle 2 heaping cups of crumb mixture, completely covering liquid. Bake at 375 °F. for 40–50 minutes or until nicely browned.

Baking Ladies, Christ Lutheran Church, Springtown, Pennsylvania

TURKEY SALAD

Serves 50.

1—14 lb. turkey, roasted   1-1/2 qts. (approx.) Miracle
1-1/3 bunches celery   Whip salad dressing
16 eggs, boiled   1—2 cups ginger ale
1 large can crushed pineapple   1 t. salt
18 oz. macaroni shells   Pepper, onion powder, and
1/2 onion, chopped   garlic salt to taste

To cook macaroni, bring salted water to a boil; add macaroni; return to boil. Cover tightly and shut off heat. Let stand 20 minutes. Drain and rinse with cold water.

Chop turkey; add rest of ingredients including pineapple juice. Salad dressing should be mixed with ginger ale until slightly thin. Add salt, pepper, onion powder, garlic salt to dressing and pour over salad. Chill at least 4 hours before serving. Can mix all except dressing the night before.

Jackie Mortenson, First Lutheran Church of Crystal, Minneapolis, Minnesota

CHICKEN RICE CASSEROLE

Serves 100.

8 qts. chicken, diced
4 qts. soft bread crumbs
   (2 sandwich loaves trimmed)
2 qts. (3 lbs.) rice, cooked
6 T. salt

4 T. pimiento
32 eggs, beaten
2 cups melted butter or
   chicken fat
6 qts. chicken stock

Mix all ingredients together. Put into three 22-1/2''x12-1/2'' greased pans. Bake at 350°F. for 1 hour. First 30 minutes should be covered; second 30 minutes uncovered. Serve with mushroom sauce.

MUSHROOM SAUCE

1—#5 can mushroom soup   Milk (equal amount of soup can)

Mix ingredients together and heat thoroughly.

Mrs. Dee McCoy, Tabernacle Presbyterian Church, Indianapolis, Indiana

CHICKEN/MUSHROOM DELIGHT

Serves 12-14.

4–5 lbs. chicken   1 large can mushrooms

Cook and bone chicken (Make lots of broth when cooking chicken). Cook mushrooms in liquid of mushrooms for 5 minutes. Mix mushrooms and chicken. Using 1-1/2–2 cups broth, make thin gravy, thickened with 2 tablespoons flour. Combine gravy with chicken/mushroom mixture and place in 9''x13'' lightly greased baking dish. Pour dressing over top of chicken mixture. Pour additional broth (approximately 2 cups) over dressing just before baking. Bake at 400°F. for 30–45 minutes or until brown.

DRESSING

1 onion
1 cup celery, diced
1-1/2 loaves bread
2 eggs

2 T. poultry seasoning
Salt
Pepper
Chicken broth

Cook together onion and celery. Tear apart bread in large bowl; add onion/celery mixture, eggs, salt and pepper to taste, and 1 tablespoon poultry seasoning. Using chicken broth, moisten bread mixture to texture of cake mix. Pour dressing over top of chicken mixture in baking pan. Pour additional broth (approximately 2 cups) over dressing just before baking.

This recipe serves 12–14 people, however, it has been multiplied and served many times at church dinners.

Mrs. Rita Harrington, St. Paul United Methodist Church, Bloomington, Indiana

BEEF STEW
Serves 125.

40 lbs. boneless chuck roast, trimmed and cut up into stew meat
40 lbs. potatoes, diced
12 bunches celery, diced
10 lbs. onions, diced
10 lbs. carrots, cut up

1 jar La Choy brown gravy sauce
6–8 qts. tomatoes
Salt and pepper to taste
Large bottle Crisco oil
Flour

Dredge meat in flour and brown in oil in heavy (or iron) skillets. Transfer meat to 4 electric roasters. Add tomatoes, cubed vegetables, brown gravy sauce, and seasonings. Cook on low heat until meat is tender and vegetables done.

Phyllis A. Taylor, Rochester Christian Church, Rochester, Illinois

HILDA HOLMES' POOR MAN'S STEAK
Serves 12, and has been served frequently to the local Rotary Club.

3 lbs. ground beef
1 cup milk
1 cup cracker crumbs

1 t. salt
2 cans cream of mushroom soup, undiluted

Mix ingredients together. Spread in dripping pan. Cut into squares. Cover and refrigerate overnight. Flour and brown each square. Return to dripping pan and add undiluted soup. Cover and bake at 350°F. for 1 hour.

Millie McGrew, United Methodist Church, Delphi, Indiana

MEAT LOAF
Serves 45–50.

9 lbs. hamburger
6 cups tomato juice
3/4 box instant oatmeal
2 cups minced onion or 2 pkgs. onion soup
9 eggs

Little water
4 T. salt
Accent
3/4 T. pepper
2 cans tomato soup, to be poured on top of loaves

Mix into large loaves and top with tomato soup. Bake at 350°F. for 1-1/2 hours.

Pat Young, First Christian Church, Quincy, Illinois

STATE FAIR CHILI

Serves 50–60, and is served every year in church's food booth at the Minnesota State Fair.

10 lbs. ground beef
4 stalks celery
5 lbs. onions
8–10 cloves garlic
2 gals. whole tomatoes
1/2 gal. tomato paste

12 t. salt
10 heaping t. chili powder
1/2 cup sugar
3 t. pepper
3 gals. kidney beans
(do not drain)

Brown beef, add chopped onions and cook until limp. Combine all other ingredients and simmer at least 2 hours, until celery is tender.

Jeanette Clonkey, Jehovah Lutheran Church, St. Paul, Minnesota

GROUND BEEF AND TATER TOT CASSEROLE

Serves 50.

8 lbs. ground beef
6 large pkgs. frozen mixed
vegetables
8 cans cream of mushroom soup, undiluted

2 large pkgs. Tater Tots
1/2 cup onion, chopped

Crumble ground beef in bottom of large roaster or baking pan. Season with salt and pepper. Spread vegetables over meat and onions; spread soup over vegetables. Place Tater Tots around on top of mixture. Bake at 400°F. until mixture is bubbling, then reduce heat to 350°F. or lower. Bake 2–2-1/2 hours.

Elva Thornburg, Christian Church (Disciples of Christ), Estherville, Iowa

HAMBURGER SUPREME

Serves 100.

20 lbs. ground beef
Salt and pepper
4-1/2 cups bread crumbs
20 eggs

1-1/4 cups Worcestershire sauce
2 cups mushroom soup
1—#5 can mushroom soup
Milk (equal to soup can)

Mix beef, seasonings, crumbs, eggs, and 2 cups soup. Form into patties or balls. Brown quickly in hot fat; drain. Mix can of soup with milk and pour over patties. Bake at 350°F. for 45 minutes.

Mrs. Dee McCoy, Tabernacle Presbyterian Church, Indianapolis, Indiana

SPAGHETTI SAUCE

Serves 150.

15 lbs. ground beef
6 gals. tomato sauce
2 cups dried onion flakes
2 t. celery seed
1 bottle Italian seasoning

6 bay leaves (remove after
  simmering)
2 t. garlic salt
Salt and pepper to taste

Brown ground beef in oven. Combine remaining ingredients and simmer 1 hour. Remove bay leaves; add browned ground beef.

Pat Young, First Christian Church, Quincy, Illinois

BARBECUED BEEF SANDWICHES

Serves 40.

6 lbs. chuck roast
1 green pepper, chopped
1 stalk celery, chopped
3 large onions, chopped
1—14 oz. bottle ketchup
3 T. barbecue sauce

3 T. vinegar
2 T. chili powder
1 T. salt
1 t. pepper
1-1/2 cups water

Brown meat well. Add all ingredients and cook in a 300°F. oven for 5–6 hours. Stir every hour and add small amount of water, if necessary. When meat is almost done, remove from pan (roaster) and remove bones; shread with fork. Return to pan and continue cooking.

Can be double or tripled. If using electric roaster, cooking time is shorter (4–5 hours). Can be frozen.

Marjorie C. Smith, Immanuel Lutheran Church, Braddock, Pennsylvania

HAM LOAF

Serves 150.

25 lbs. meat (17 lbs. ham and
  8 lbs. fresh pork)
25 eggs, beaten well

1 qt. unsalted cracker crumbs
1-1/2 qts. warm milk

Mix crumbs with meat; add eggs, then milk. Mix well and shape into loaves. Bake covered with foil at 350°F. for 1 hour. Pour off liquid, remove foil; bake another 40 minutes.

SAUCE

1 qt. mayonnaise
1 qt. sour cream
1/2 cup sugar

1/4 cup mustard
1 jar horseradish

Mix and serve with ham loaf.

Mrs. Dee McCoy, Tabernacle Presbyterian Church, Indianapolis, Indiana

JOY'S HAM LOAF SPECIAL

Used for many luncheons, receptions, and banquets.

3 lbs. ground smoked ham	3 T. dehydrated minced onion
1-1/2 lbs. ground fresh pork	3/4 cup milk
24 square crackers, crushed	3 eggs
(about 1-1/2 cups)	Dash pepper

Thoroughly combine all ingredients and shape into 2 loaves. Bake at 325°F. for 30 minutes. Combine glaze mixture and pour over loaves, baking additional 60 minutes. Baste occasionally. Yield: 16–18 slices each.

GLAZE

2 cups brown sugar	2 T. vinegar
1/3 cup pineapple juice	2 t. mustard

Combine ingredients and pour over loaves.

Joy Crawford, Eureka Presbyterian Church, Eureka, Illinois

HAMMETTES

Serves 50.

5 lbs. ground ham	2-1/2 cups vinegar
7-1/2 lbs. ground pork	7-1/2 cups brown sugar
5 cups crushed cracker crumbs	2-1/2 cups water
5 cups milk	2-1/2 t. ground mustard
10 eggs	

Combine ground ham, pork, cracker crumbs, milk, and eggs. Mix together well, then form into small loaves about the size of your fist. Place in a roasting pan. Combine vinegar, brown sugar, water, and mustard. Bring all ingredients to a boil, then pour over hammettes. Bake at 325°F. for 1-1/2 hours. Baste often with pan juices. Makes 50 hammettes.

One 1 pound box of saltine crackers yields 4 cups crumbs. One 2 pound bag of brown sugar yields 4-2/3 cups.

United Methodist Women, United Methodist Church, Milledgeville, Illinois

Index

Everybody's Favorites Order Form

Everybody's Favorites cookbook is a unique collection of the very best, most requested recipes from churches throughout the United States and Canada. It includes favorites from church potlucks, receptions, coffee hours, bake sales, picnics, congregational dinners, banquets, fellowship events, luncheons and teas. Order your copy (or additional copies) by returning this order form. *Payment must be enclosed with order.*

Quantity	Item	Price Each	Total
	Everybody's Favorites Cookbook	$7.95	$
	Ohio Residents add 5% sales tax		
	Shipping & Handling (regardless of quantity)	$	2.00
	Total Order	$	

Ship To:
Name _____
Address _____
City _____ State_____Zip_____

☐ *Send quantity prices and complete information on how my organization can use this cookbook as a fund raiser.*

Make checks payable to: **Communication Resources**
P.O. Box 2625
North Canton, OH 44720
216/499-1950

Everybody's Favorites: The Perfect Fundraiser

Please send quantity prices and complete information on how my organization can use **Everybody's Favorites** cookbook as a fundraiser.

Name _____

Address _____

City _____ State_____ Zip_____

Name of your organization_____

Communication Resources
P.O. Box 2625
North Canton, OH 44720
216/499-1950

From:

_____

_____

_____

Place
Stamp
Here

Communication Resources
P.O. Box 2625
North Canton, OH 44720